Magical Symbolism

Runes, Bindrunes, Galdrastafir, and Astrological Symbols for Magic

Matthew Leigh Embleton

For a list of books by the author please visit:
www.matthewleighembleton.co.uk

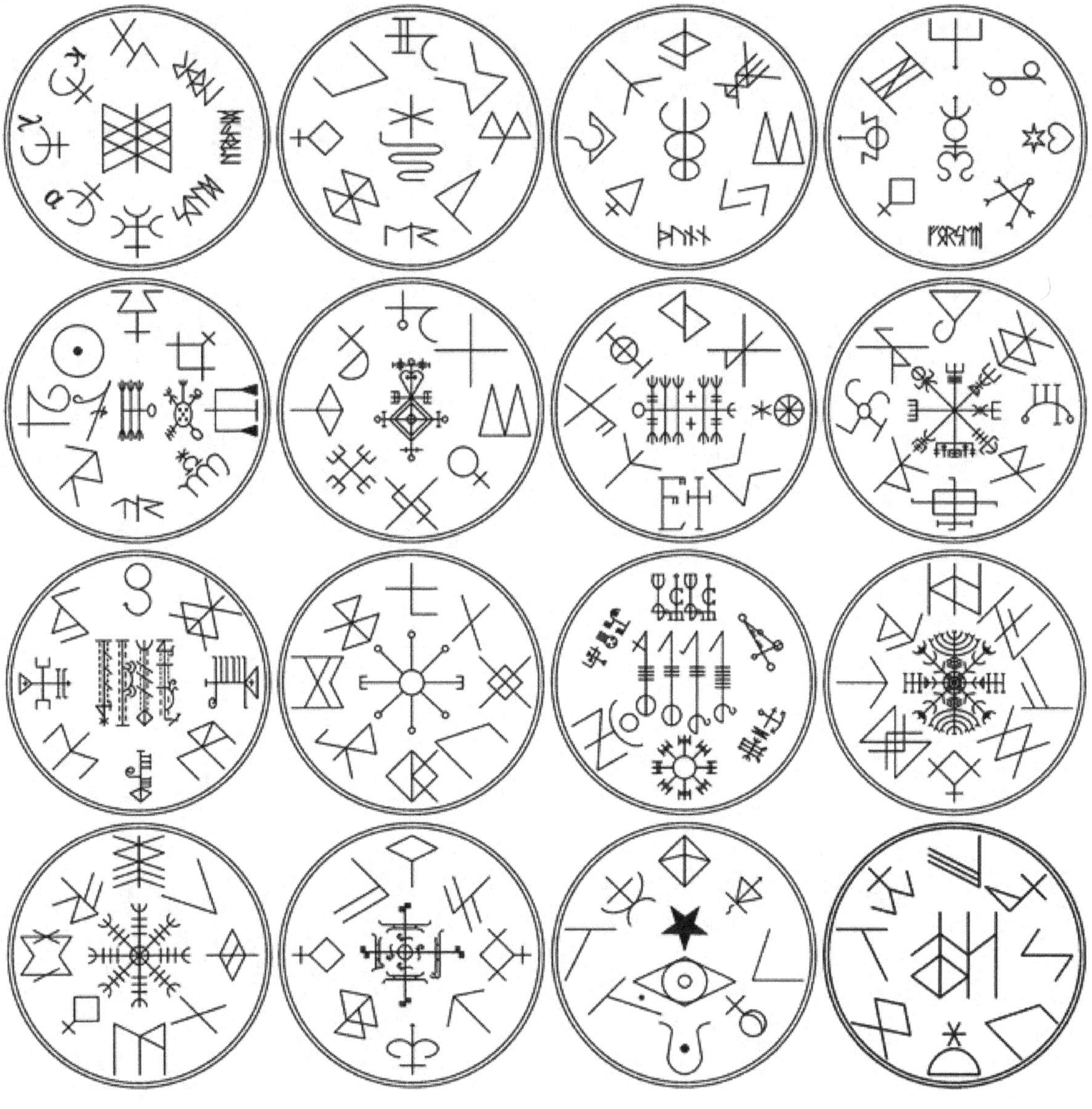

Copyright ©2022 Matthew Leigh Embleton. All rights reserved.

Magical Symbolism

1. Runes 1
2. Bindrunes 9
3. Bindrunes for Norse Deities 26
4. Staves and Symmetry 34
5. Galdrastafir 36
6. Astrological Symbols 89
7. Shields 113
   - 7.1 Divine Inspiration 113
   - 7.2 Fate and Destiny 115
   - 7.3 Fertility 116
   - 7.4 Health and Wellbeing 118
   - 7.5 Justice 119
   - 7.6 Love 121
   - 7.7 Luck 122
   - 7.8 Music and Art 123
   - 7.9 Protection 124
   - 7.10 Resolving Conflict 125
   - 7.11 Setting Intentions 126
   - 7.12 Sleep and Dreams 127
   - 7.13 Strength 128
   - 7.14 Success and Victory 129
   - 7.15 The Sea 130
   - 7.16 Wealth 130
   - 7.17 Wisdom 131
8. The Misuse of Runes: What to Avoid 133

Cover: A selection of magical shields, created by the author

Acknowledgments

I have long been fascinated by languages and history, and I am very grateful to the special people in my life who have supported and encouraged me in my work. Thank you for believing in me. You know who you are.

Introduction

In such times of increasing misunderstanding, incomplete information, misinformation, and misguided criticism, it has become necessary to add a number of clarifications in order to set the record straight in this expanded introduction.

The Viking Age and North Germanic Paganism

In recent decades popular culture has rediscovered the Viking Age and North Germanic Paganism with fresh eyes. From the pirates and sea raiders known as Vikings, to the fierce warriors called Berserkers, and the wider Norse or Nordic people as a whole, symbols played an important role in daily life and spirituality.

Today we find these symbols visually eye catching and their meanings fascinating. People all over the world are finding meaning in these symbols that resonate with their personality, identity, and spiritual beliefs.

Symbols for personal magic

These symbols are a representation of a thought or an idea, from a single line to an ever increasingly complex symmetry of lines, circles, intersecting lines, and bold striking angles. Perhaps one of the most popular of these symbols is the Vegvísir, one of the many Galdrastafir (praying or chanting staves) that appeared in Iceland after its settlement by Norse people in the late 9th century, but there are many many more.

Manuscript sources of Galdrastafir

The word 'manuscript' comes from the Medieval Latin '*manuscriptum*', which came from the Latin '*manu*' = by hand + '*scriptus*' = written. In the Norse tradition they are called '*handrit*' = hand written. The manuscripts that have survived contain a wealth of magical symbols drawn by hand in what were personal handbooks called '*galdrabók*' ('*galdra*' = spells, magic, or incantations + '*bók*' = book or '*bókir*' = books). Sometimes they are called a *grimoire* or *grimoires*, a term used restrospectively which is believed to be of Old French origin, referring to the tradition of manuscripts in Latin.

These *galdrabókir* were the result of collected and shared knowledge within a community of practitioners of magic, often in secrecy. For a while it was illegal to own such a book, and so they were kept hidden and remained for the personal use of the owner in their persona collection. They may well have been used as a reference to teach the tradition to initiates, but the idea that in their written form they were designed to be purely instructional on their own and read like a catalogue without any guidance by an elder is a false one.

As anyone who like myself has trawled through these manuscripts will tell you, in some cases there are accompanying sentences explaining the meaning and instruction on the use of each symbol, and in many cases the very name of the symbol told the owner all they needed to know.

From the name or title of the symbol, how that symbol was used was a matter of personal choice, depending on the circumstances and the type of incantation or spell that was to be performed. This use would have been guided by the person's own understanding of the nature and the spirit of magic, of signalling their intentions to the universe.

A single symbol in a *galdrabók* is called a '*galdrastafr*' = galdra or galdor stave. The plural is *galdrastafir*, therefore the plural term 'galdrastafirs' with the plural -s suffix is incorrect, as the term *galdrastafir* is already plural.

Runes

The meaning of the word 'rune' comes from the Germanic root '*run-*' meaning '*secret*' or '*whisper*'. Similar versions of this word are also found in Old Irish Gaelic, Welsh, Old English (Anglo-Saxon), Baltic languages such as Lithuanian, and also Finnish, with such meanings as '*intention*', '*miracle*', '*mystery*', '*poem*', '*scratched letter*', '*secret*', '*secret writing*', '*speech*', '*to carve*', '*to speak*', and '*whisper*', which collectively suggest a common connection over a broad spectrum of meaning reaching far back into time. These runes are the basic building blocks of meaning which can either be used on their own, or configured into bindrunes.

Bindrunes

A bindrune or '*bindrúna*' (plural = bindrunes '*bindrúnir*') is a combination of two or more runes into a single symbol, by varying degrees of overlapping and symmetrical configuration, to compound and amplify meaning and significance. It can be used to either exaggerate or obscure the meanings of the symbols used.

Bindrunes are mentioned in the *Sigrdrífumál* which is part of the Poetic Edda (overlapping two Tyr runes and carving them on to a sword for victory). The Poetic Edda is one of the most important documents of Old Norse religion and mythology, which is known to have formed at least as far back as the Proto-Norse period (2nd to 8th centuries CE), preserved in the Codex Regius during the 1270s.

Bindrunes have been adopted by many modern traditions, revivals of traditions, syncretic traditions, religious movements, and occultist Western esoterica, including Wicca, but they are neither owned nor govered by any of them.

A large number of simple bindrunes have been popularised and widely disseminated into these modern traditions in many circles. They have been carved, burned, engraved, or even printed on to all manner of personal items by craftspeople all over the world, and such items are a valuable introduction into the idea of personal talismanic magic.

These popular bindrunes are included in this book as reference, but they are by no means the only ones available, and to describe them as being 'wicca' in nature is incorrect. They are part of an ancient tradition and they exist by invention and for the purpose of invention, through the creativity of the individuals who formulate them and use them.

As well as considering the design of these bindrunes, the reader is also encouraged to consider formulating their own personal bindrune or bindrunes, using the runes as building blocks, using the basic principle of symmetry described in this book or not, as is their personal choice.

The misuse of symbols

Galdrastafir have been associated with the misuse of runes and Norse symbols as a whole. In 2019 reports emerged claiming that depictions of runes and Norse symbols, including those represented in traditional Viking jewellery, may soon be banned in Sweden, including *Mjolnir* (Thor's Hammer), the *Valknut*, and the *Vegvísir* ('way-seer' / 'way marker' / Nordic compass).

For the last 120 years, runes and other Norse symbols have been misguidedly misused, misrepresented, and misinterpreted by some, as part of systems of propaganda for extreme and objectionable political agendas. This form of cultural appropriation has done great damage in obscuring and twisting the original and true meanings of the runes.

The misuse of runes by the Nazis is well documented and well known, but sadly this knowledge is sometimes inadvertently misused by people who in their noble fight against objectionable political ideas and their association with historical atrocities end up losing their way, equating this misuse of runes with that of a 2,000 year old tradition which is experienced innocently by pagans and spiritualists around the world, who have been mistakenly and undeservedly reviled as being associated with ideas and beliefs that they do not have and find abhorrent as much as the next person.

The 'Othala' or 'Odal' rune

One particular example is the 'Othala' or 'Odal' rune, which is perhaps the easiest of runes to have its meaning distorted in this way since it represents the idea of ancestry and homeland. There are two versions of this symbol, one with 'feet' or 'wings' and one without. The version without these 'wings' or 'feet' is the older of the two and is found in the majority of Futharks.

The version with 'wings' or 'feet' comes from its traditional use as a regular pattern of interlocking Othala runes, the right way up and upside down contiguously, around the circumference of property, such as the wall of a house, or a fence around a piece of land.

This version of the rune has also been used as an astrological symbol for Asteroid #3989 known as 'Odin' discovered on 8th September 1986 by P Jensen at the Brorfelde Observatory in Denmark. The name and number of this asteroid was allocated by the Minor Planet Center (MPC) which is part of the Smithsonian Astrophysical Observatory. All of this has been overlooked in favour of the idea that it was exclusively used by the Nazis.

A clear difference in the Nazi use of the 'Othala' or 'Odal' rune along with the rest of the runes is the bold, thick, and lines with thick squared corners, rather than the thin lines that one would normally see in runes that are carved or written.

Perhaps the most difficult way of innocently representing this rune would be in the form of a pendant in which the rune appears on its own without any backing, since a degree of thickness would be needed in order to provide rigidity and durability to avoid it being bent or broken. There are anecdotal accounts in discussion forums on the internet describing how people have punitively snatched such pendants from around the necks of wearers exclaiming "Nazis wear these!"... to which the correct answer must be... "...*and so do millions of innocent pagans!*".

Hate symbols

The Anti-Defamation League has an online database of hate symbols containing runes misused by Nazis and far-right groups, rightly stating that because these runes continue "to be used by non-racists, typically adherents of neo-pagan religions, one should not simply assume that a particular use of this symbol is racist, but should carefully judge it in its context".

Conclusion

By discovering these magical symbols, you are rightly reaffirming the true meaning of their culture. Not only that but in true spirit you are refusing to allow access to this culture to be denied to you by those who mistakenly believe that the misuse of these symbols is their only use. Such people seeking to revile and punish innocent users of pagan symbols are actually enabling far right organisations to steal this culture.

The magic of the Norse people worked because they believed that it worked. They believed in the process of signalling and communicating their intentions and desirable outcomes to the forces around them, projecting them into the universe, and having the confidence and belief to make things happen.

1. Runes

Runes are a set of letters in a series of runic alphabets or 'futharks' which are believed to have evolved from the Italic alphabets used in the Italian peninsula during the Roman Imperial period (1st century B.C.E to 5th Century C.E), which spread into Northern Europe and evolved in different directions. During this time they were imbued with a sense of magical and mythological significance beyond their literal linguistic meaning, which found its way into literature, including the story of how Odin sacrificed himself on the world tree Yggdrasil in order to gain knowledge and mastery of the runes in the Hávamál (sayings of the high one, Odin).

This is a list of the common runes that appear in various forms in the Elder Futhark, Younger Futhark, Anglo-Saxon Futhorc, and Icelandic Futhark, listed with their magical uses and intentions.

Symbol	Name(s)
ᚠ	Fehu, Feoh, Fe Energy projection and sending energy, drawing energy, increasing wealth, protecting valuables, increasing libido
ᚢ	Uruz, Ur Initiation, healing, shaping and forming of desire, will, knowledge of the self
ᚦ	Thurisaz, Thorn, Thurs New beginnings, luck in circumstances beyond your control, guarding and protection, awakening the magical will
ᚨ ᚫ ᚬ	Ansuz, Os, As, Oss Magical incantation, convincing and magnetic speech, gaining wisdom, and divine communication, finding the truth in the matter, increasing magical energies

Magical Symbolism   *1. Runes*

Symbol	Name(s)
ᚱ	Raido, Rad, Reid Moral justice, rhythm and timing, ordered movement, travel
ᚲ	Kaunan, Cen, Kaun Protection from and healing of wounds, love, stability and passion in relationships, releases spirit into the realms of power, protection of valuables
ᚷ	Gebo, Gyfu Love magic, endless exchange of energy and magical powers, mystical union, binding, a gift for a gift, karmic payback
ᚹ	Wunjo, Wynn Personal happiness and fulfilment, healing relationships, success in travel
ᚺ	Hagalaz, Haegl, Hagall Completeness and bringing into being, warding, protection, luck, encouraging a positive result

2

Magical Symbolism   1. Runes

Symbol	Name(s)
	Naudiz, Nyd, Naudr, Naud Overcoming fate and stress, developing magical will, sudden inspiration and inner might, achieving goals, to find a lover or to encourage a relationship
	Isaz, Is, Isa, Iss Strengthening concentration and will, maintaining something as it is, binding, holding on to something, halting movement
	Stung-Inn Is To thaw a freeze, to navigate difficult and bleak conditions
	Jera, Ger, Ar Patience and natural harmony of magical will, spiritual understanding, creative planning, interactions with nature and natural time cycles, promoting healing
	Aesa Nourishment, Longevity, Survival
	Ihwaz, Eoh Initiation, wisdom from past lives, increasing power and store power, spirit communication, removal of obstacles

Magical Symbolism   1. Runes

Symbol	Name(s)
⟁	Perth, Peorth Divination, perception of fate, to manifest magical intent, use when dealing with matters of speculation, finding lost things, good mental health
ᛉ	Algiz, Ilx Protection from evil and enemies, strengthening luck and life force, communication and connection with guardian spirit, spiritual cleansing, strengthen magical power, travelling through other worlds, astral travel
ᛊ / ᛋ / ϟ (variants)	Sowilo, Sigel, Sol Strengthening magical spiritual will, guardianship and guidance, personal triumph, success, healing, increasing strength and self confidence, survival, rebirth and re-creation
ᛏ	Tiwaz, Tir, Tyr Victory and justice, strength in competition, defence magic, to strengthen with spiritual and moral force
ᛐ (stung)	Stung-Inn Tyr Victory and justice, strength in competition, defence magic, to strengthen with spiritual and moral force
╪	Dis Sorcery, Magic Arts

Magical Symbolism   1. Runes

Symbol	Name(s)
ᛒ	Berkanan, Beorc, Bjork, Bjarkan, Bjarken
	Fertility magic, protection, concealment and secrecy, family matters, to bring into being
ᛒ (dotted)	Plastur
	Care, Relief, Remedy, Healing, Curing of Wounds, Amelioration of the Mind
ᛖ	Ehwaz, Eh
	Bringing swift change, safe travel, shamanic totem animal, mystical wisdom, projecting and linking magical thoughts, cooperation
ᛘ ᛉ	Mannaz, Mann, Madr, Madur
	Strengthening all matters of the mind and psychic ability, balanced through meditation, increasing mental power and memory, to gain help from others, comfort, voice, wordsmithery, poetry
ᛚ	Laguz, Lagu, Logr, Logur
	Increasing and filling yourself with life-force and intuition, probing the subconscious and the unknown, physical and magical strength and vitality
ᛜ ᛝ	Ingwaz, Ing
	Storing, transferring or releasing magical power and energy, to keep a thing hidden, fertility, to bring a satisfactory conclusion
ᛟ	Othala, Ethel
	Strengthening the clan, family including spiritual ancestry, to gain past life wisdom, talents, to gain wealth and protect what you own, to protect the health of an elderly person

Magical Symbolism   1. Runes

Symbol	Name(s)
	Dagaz, Daeg Becoming one with the universe through mystical inspiration, a change of attitude in yourself or someone else, synthesis of opposites into a single concept such as light and dark, financial increase
	Ac Order, Gods, Oak
	Aesc Order, Gods, Ash Tree
	Yr Protection from evil and enemies, strengthening luck and life force, communication and connection with guardian spirit, spiritual cleansing, strengthen magical power, travelling through other worlds, astral travel, death initiation, wisdom from past lives, increasing power and store power, spirit communication
	Ior Serpent, Dual Nature, Hardships
	Ear Earth, Endings, Life and Death
	Calc Chalice, Endings

Magical Symbolism   *1. Runes*

Symbol	Name(s)
	Gar, Gungnir The spear of Odin
	Cweorth Fire, Flame, Transformation
	Stan Stone, Obstructions
	Elli Longevity, Sanctuary, Surviving Difficulty

Magical Symbolism   *1. Runes*

The Web of Urðr

The Web of Urðr (also known in Anglo-Saxon as 'Wyrd') is the common name for a powerful symbol out of which all runes can be found. It contains 9 interlocking lines, representing the 9 worlds, but also representing the web itself, out of which all things (in this case runes) are made possible.

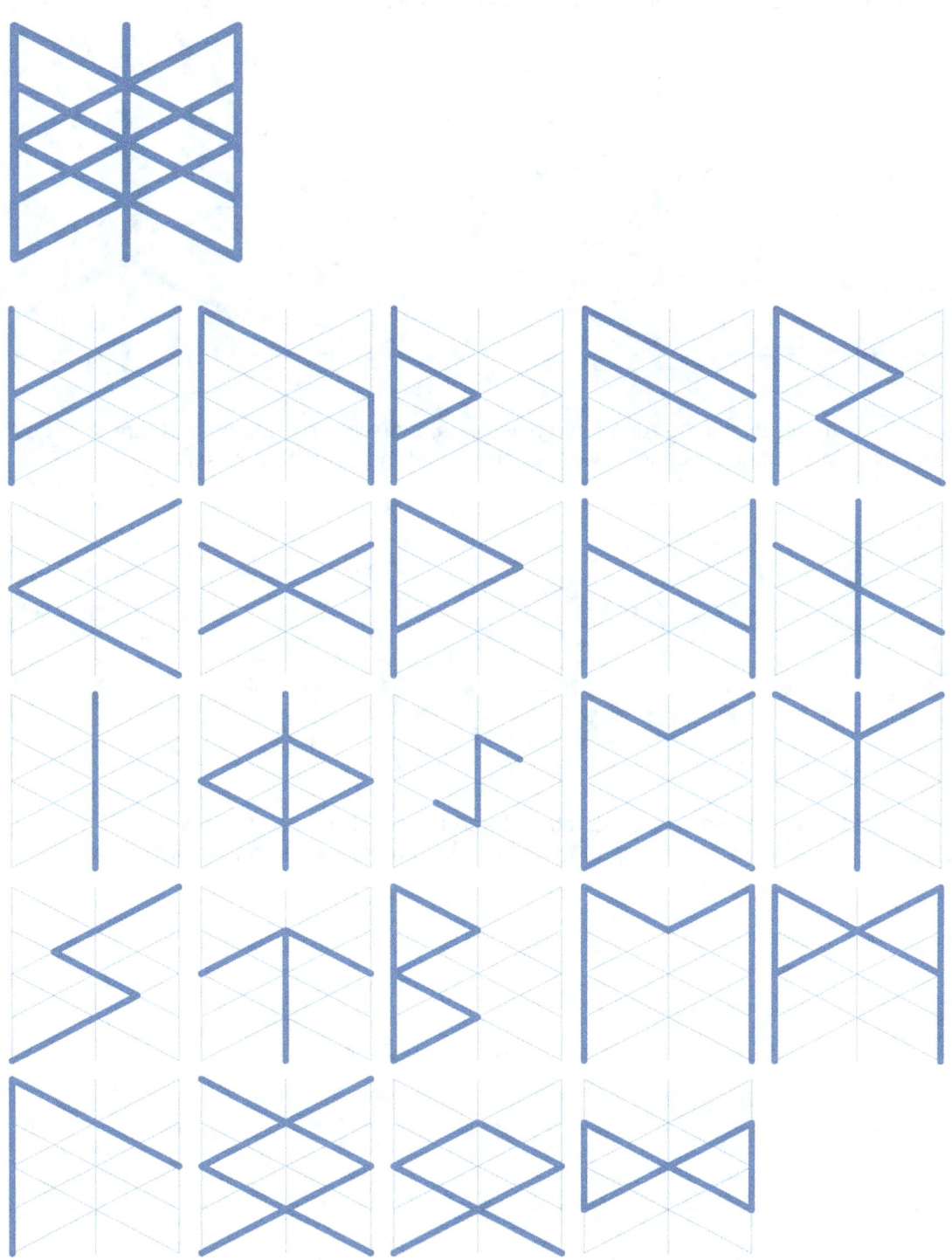

2. Bindrunes

A bindrune is a combination of two or more runes into a single symbol, by varying degrees of overlapping and symmetrical configuration, to compound and amplify meaning and significance. It can be used to either exaggerate or obscure the meanings of the symbols used.

Example:

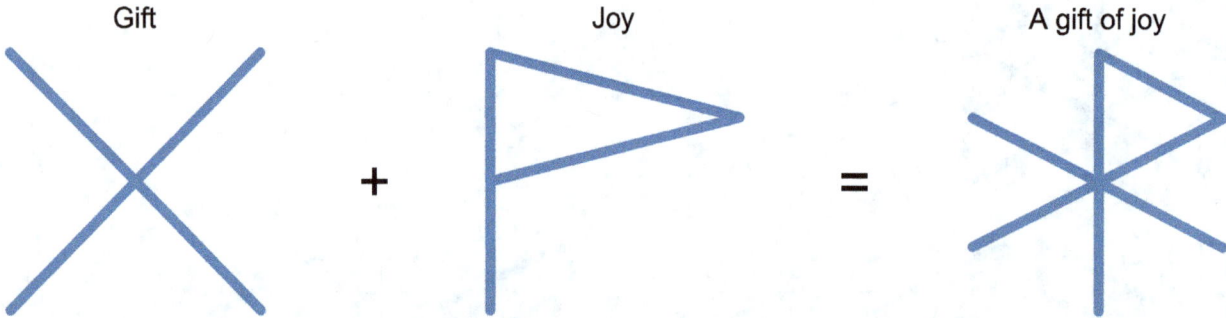

Make sure that while you are combining runes into bindrunes, there are no unintended runes that can also be inadvertently found that could undo or work against what the symbol represents.

Example:

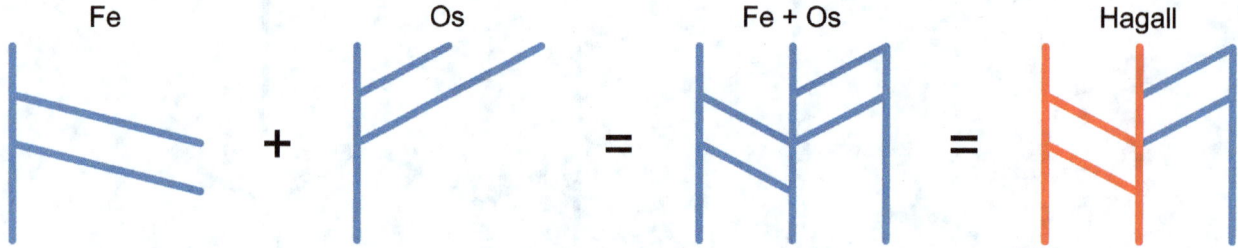

There is no limit to how many runes can be combined into a bindrune, or to the number of points of symmetry you can use, from a simple overlap of two runes, to large elaborate and intricate staves.

Magical Symbolism   *2. Bindrunes*

Symbol	Name	Meaning
	Creation	A combination of the younger Fuþark letters 'Mathr' meaning 'Man', and a version of 'As' meaning 'Æsir', the principal pantheon of the Norse gods, symbolising the creation of man and his relationship with the gods.
	Inspiration	A combination of 'Ingwaz' referring to the god Freyr, 'Kaunan', a torch or fire, 'Ihwaz' for strength, and slow steady growth.
	Creativity	A combination of 'Wunjo' for joy and harmony, 'Laguz' representing dreams and fantasies, and several versions of a torch 'Kaunan' (Elder Fuþark), 'Kaun' (Younger Fuþark), and 'Cen' (Anglo-Saxon).
	Divine energy	A combination of 'Tiwaz' meaning 'Tyr', the Norse warrior god, strengthening spiritual and moral force, and two mirrored versions of the younger Fuþark 'As' meaning 'Æsir', the principal pantheon of the Norse gods.
	Ready power, instant deployment	A combination of two 'Uruz' runes overlapped, 'Uruz' represents a wild ox, physical strength, speed, untamed potential, primal strength, force, vitality, and masculinity, which can be used for healing, and knowledge of the self.

Magical Symbolism 2. Bindrunes

Symbol	Name	Meaning
	Energy	A combination of the rune 'Raido', movement or movement of energy, and a version of the younger Fuþark 'As' meaning 'Æsir', the principal pantheon of the Norse gods.
	Fertility, taking root, beginning growth	A combination of 'Ihwaz', a tree and slow steady growth, 'Ehwaz', change and team work, and 'Dagaz', dawn, a breakthrough, awakening, embarking on an enterprise, and new beginnings.
	Growth and fertility	A combination of the younger Fuþark 'Yr', a yew tree or slow steady growth, and 'Bjarken', a birch tree, birth, fertility, growth, and bringing into being.
	Happy family and marriage	This is an overlapping of several 'Hagalaz' runes, which can be used for magical purposes for completeness, bringing into being, and warding or protection.
	Balanced joy	This is a double image of the 'Wunjo' rune, with one acting as the mirror of the other, meaning joy, comfort, pleasure, good fortune, delight, happiness, fellowship, and harmony.

Magical Symbolism 2. *Bindrunes*

Symbol	Name	Meaning
	A gift of joy	This is a combination of the rune 'Gebo' meaning gift, and 'Wunjo' meaning joy (square version).
	A gift of joy	This is a combination of the rune 'Gebo' meaning gift, and 'Wunjo' meaning joy (hexagonal version).
	Lasting partnership	This is a combination of the rune 'Ingwaz', meaning internal growth, love, caring, and gentleness, and the rune 'Isaz' for binding together.
	Longevity and perseverance	This is a combination of the rune 'Dagaz', breakthrough or embarking on an enterprise, with the rune 'Isaz' for binding.
	Enhancing athletic performance	This is a combination of the rune 'Ehwaz', physical movement, 'Uruz', physical strength, speed, untamed potential and vitality, and 'Sowilo', the sun, success, goals realised, honour, perfection, and health.

Magical Symbolism   *2. Bindrunes*

Symbol	Name	Meaning
	Good health	This is a combination of 'Laguz' meaning water and the power of renewal and healing, also increasing and filling yourself with a life force, and physical and magical strength, and 'Thurisaz' used for protection and warding.
	Grace and gracefulness	This is a combination of the rune 'Wunjo' meaning joy and harmony, and a version of the younger Fuþark 'As' meaning 'Æsir', the principal pantheon of the Norse gods.
	Health & healing	This is a combination of 'Laguz', water, the power of renewal, and healing, 'Berkano', renewal and rebirth, and 'Algiz' meaning a shield of protection.
	Health & healing	This is a combination of 'Kenaz', vital fire of life, 'Ihwaz', strength and reliability, and 'Sowilo', perfect health, all is well.
	Help giving up bad habits	This is a combination of 'Othala', where your heart lies, 'Kenaz', the vital fire of life and determination, and 'Jera', patience, natural harmony of magical will.

Magical Symbolism 2. Bindrunes

Symbol	Name	Meaning
	Medical healing	This is a combination of 'Berkano', renewal, nurturing, 'Algiz', strengthening protection, and 'Laguz', the power of renewal and healing.
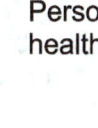	Personal good health	A combination of the rune 'Raido', movement or movement of energy, two 'Isaz' binding verticals, and a version of the younger Fuþark 'As' meaning 'Æsir', the principal pantheon of the Norse gods.
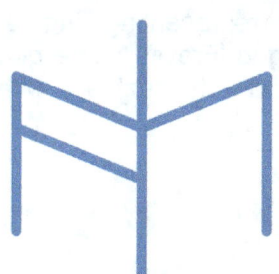	Restoring balance	'Ansuz', divine communication, finding the truth, 'Algiz', communication and connection with a guardian spirit, spiritual cleansing, and 'Ehwaz', harmony, soul travel, a shamanic totem, and overcoming of obstacles.
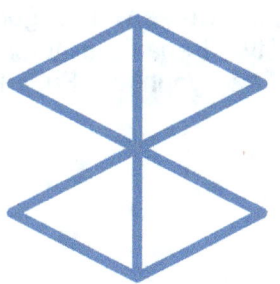	Vitality	This is a combination of two 'Berkano' runes mirrored side by side, representing renewal and vitality.
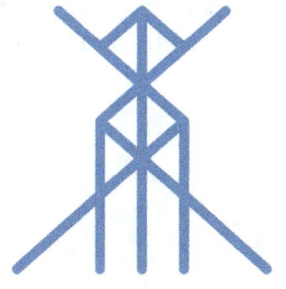	Vitality	This complex and powerful bind rune is a combination of 'Ingwaz', fertility, internal growth, 'Berkano', vitality and wellbeing, 'Algiz', protection, 'Uruz', strength and energy.

Magical Symbolism   2. Bindrunes

Symbol	Name	Meaning
	Youth and youthfulness	This is a combination of a version of the younger Fuþark rune 'Yr', a yew tree, a symbol of rebirth, and a medieval version of the rune 'Àr' meaning a harvest and a good year.
	Eternal love	This is a combination of 'Gebo', gifts, relationship, partnership, blessing, balance, giving and exchanging, and union, and 'Jera', peace, prosperity, fruitful harvest, and harmony of magical will.
	Charm for a man towards a man	This is a version of 'Ingwaz', representing 'Ing' or 'Yngvi', another name for the god 'Freyr', Norse god of peace and male fertility, bound with 'Isaz', and with all lines reaching outwards.
	Charm for a man towards a woman	A combination 'Tiwaz', honour, the Norse warrior god Tyr, 'Ihwaz', strength, reliability, 'Kenaz', a torch, passion, determination, and the younger Fuþark 'Mathr', man.
	Charm for a woman towards a man	A combination of 'Ingwaz', an opening, love and gentleness, 'Kenaz', a torch, passion, control of sexual energy.

Magical Symbolism 2. Bindrunes

Symbol	Name	Meaning
	Charm for a woman towards a woman	A combination of 'Ingwaz', an opening, love and gentleness, several mirrored 'Berkano' runes for nurturing and fertility magic.
	Love	This is a combination of a version of the younger Fuþark runes 'Yr', a yew tree, a symbol of rebirth, renewal, and trust, and a version of the rune 'As' meaning 'Æsir', the principal pantheon of the Norse gods.
	Good luck and good fortune	This is a combination of the rune 'Gebo', a gift, a blessing, giving and exchanging, and 'Ansuz', meaning 'Æsir', the principal pantheon of the Norse gods.
	Good luck and good fortune	This is a combination of 'Jeran', a good year, peace, prosperity, a fruitful harvest, and 'Isaz' used as a binding rune to hold in place and secure it.
	Good luck and good fortune	This is a combination of the younger Fuþark 'Fe', wealth, luck, energy, foresight, a version of 'Bjarken', new beginnings, and a version of 'As' meaning 'Æsir', the principal pantheon of the Norse gods.

Magical Symbolism 2. Bindrunes

Symbol	Name	Meaning
	Protection against evil magic	This is a combination of 'Ihwaz', a yew tree, strength, reliability, trustworthiness, knowledge, and 'Thurisaz', a thorn, a reactive force, defence, protection, a warning.
	Defence	This is a combination of 'Tiwaz', the Norse warrior god 'Tyr', justice and protection, and heroic glory, and 'Othala', strengthening and connecting with spiritual ancestry, and strengthening and protecting what is yours.
	Elimination of obstacles	This is a combination of 'Ingwaz', meaning an opening or opportunity, bound together with 'Uruz', untamed potential and the strength of a wild ox.
	Protection of home and property	This is a combination of 'Othala', heritage, home, your land of birth, your ancestry, and protection of what is yours, and 'Algiz', a shield, warding off evil, an invisible barrier, giving protection, and strengthening spiritual will.
	Personal protective power	This is a combination of several 'Algiz' runes, spiritual cleansing and connection with a guardian spirit for protection, and 'Ingwaz', for storing and transferring magical power.

Magical Symbolism   2. *Bindrunes*

Symbol	Name	Meaning
	Return ill will to the originator	This is a combination of 'Hagalaz', used for completeness and bringing into being, and for warding and protection, and a version of 'Sowilo', strengthening magical spiritual will, and success.
	Securing justice	This is a combination of 'Tiwaz', the Norse warrior god 'Tyr', honour, justice, authority, strengthening spiritual and moral force, 'Reith', a spiritual journey, evolution, and planning, bound together with opposing alternative versions of 'Tyr'.
	Protection for a vehicle	This is a combination of 'Algiz' for protection, 'Ihwaz', the yew tree, strength and reliability, trustworthiness, and 'Kenaz', vision and technical ability.
	Protection	This is a combination of 'Algiz', a shield, protection, warding off evil, an impenetrable barrier, and 'Thurisaz', a thorn, a reactive force, warding and defence, changes, and warning, awakening the magical will.
	Assertiveness	This is a combination of 'Tiwaz', Tyr, the Norse warrior god of justice, authority, and heroic glory, and 'Thurisaz', awakening the magical will.

Magical Symbolism   2. Bindrunes

Symbol	Name	Meaning
	Binding power and personal magnetism	This is a combination of the Anglo-Saxon rune 'Stan', meaning stone, 'Iar', strength and reliability, storing power, and 'Nyd', to bind, or hold on to.
	Boosting self esteem	This is a combination of 'Ehwaz', mystical wisdom, projecting and linking magical thoughts, cooperation, and 'Mannaz', strengthening all matters of the mind and psychic ability, balanced through meditation.
	Determination	This is a combination of 'Uruz', strength, untamed potential, 'Nauthiz', self-reliance, overcoming stress, inner might, and 'Ehwaz', a shamanic totem, mystical wisdom, projecting and linking magical thoughts, cooperation.
	Discipline	This is a combination of the Anglo-Saxon rune 'Jear', meaning strength and reliability, and 'Nyd', holding on to something, binding to something, limitations.
	Discovery of hidden knowledge	This is a combination of 'Perthro', representing mysteries, secrets, the unknown, the occult (that which is hidden), and 'Ansuz', insight, true vision, a secret discovered, finding the truth in the matter.

Magical Symbolism 2. Bindrunes

Symbol	Name	Meaning
	Endurance	This is a combination of 'Uruz', strength, untamed potential, 'Nauthiz', self-reliance, overcoming stress, endurance, and inner might.
	Farsightedness	This is a combination of 'Kenaz', a torch or vision, and 'Algiz', communication and connection with a guardian spirit, travelling through other worlds.
	Following dreams and passions	This is a combination of 'Laguz', representing water, dreams, and fantasies, 'Ihwaz', strength, reliability, slow steady growth, and knowledge, and a version of 'Ingwaz', internal growth, going forward, opening or an opportunity.
	Heart and realising ambition	This is a combination of the younger Fuþark rune 'Reith' two mirrored side by side, representing travel, a journey, and evolution, and 'Nauthir' representing wants and needs, overcoming, developing magical will, inspiration and might.
	Hope	This is a combination of two 'Tiwaz' runes overlapped, the Norse warrior god Tyr, divine justice, authority, honour, and heroic glory, and 'Uruz', healing, shaping and forming of desire or will, with knowledge of the self.

Magical Symbolism 2. Bindrunes

Symbol	Name	Meaning
	Inspiration	This is a combination of 'Laguz', water, dreams, fantasies, probing the subconscious and the unknown, and 'Uruz', healing, shaping and forming of desire or will, and knowledge of the self.
	Music	This is a combination of a version of the younger Fuþark rune 'Yr', a yew tree, a symbol of rebirth, and several overlapping versions of 'As', representing divine communication, and 'Æsir', the principal pantheon of the Norse gods.
	Peace, tranquillity and unity	This is a combination of 'Raido', a spiritual journey, ordered movement, 'Berkano', renewal and nurturing, and 'Laguz', water, going with the flow.
	Perseverance and everlastingness	This is a combination of 'Ingwaz', gestation, internal growth, love, caring, gentleness, storing or transferring magical power, and 'Dagaz', breakthrough, embarking on an enterprise, mystical inspiration.
	Quick results and rapid action	This is a combination of 'Raido', the chariot, travel, evolution, rhythm and timing, movement, and 'Laguz', increasing and filling yourself with life force, physical and magical strength.

Magical Symbolism 2. Bindrunes

Symbol	Name	Meaning
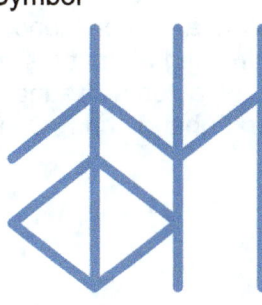	Wisdom	This is a combination of a version of 'Jeran', the yew tree, steady growth of knowledge, 'Sowilo', guidance and triumph, 'Algiz', spiritual cleansing, and connection and communication with a guardian spirit.
	Emotional strength	This is a combination of 'Uruz', strength and vitality, 'Ehwaz', mystical wisdom, linking magical thoughts, 'Laguz', water, healing emotions, magical strength.
	Health & wellbeing	This is a combination of 'Gebo', balance, an endless exchange of energy, and 'Algiz', spiritual cleansing, strengthening magical power, and protection.
	Spiritual and mental power	This is a combination of 'Mannaz', intelligence and confidence, capability, and creative skill, and 'Ansuz', divine communication, and 'Æsir', the principal pantheon of the Norse gods.
	Academic brilliance	This is a combination of two 'Ansuz' runes overlapped, to double this rune's properties of insight, communication, true vision, and finding the truth in the matter. Ansuz also means 'Æsir', the principal pantheon of the Norse gods.

Magical Symbolism   *2. Bindrunes*

Symbol	Name	Meaning
	Success in exams	This is a combination of 'Mannaz', confidence, intelligence, creative skill, strengthening all matters of the mind, and several versions of a torch 'Kaunan' (Elder Fuþark), 'Kaun' (Younger Fuþark), and 'Cen' (Anglo-Saxon).
	Success in legal matters	This is a combination of 'Raido', moral justice, movement, travel, and 'Tiwaz', the Norse warrior god Tyr, honour, justice, authority, strengthening spiritual and moral force.
	Success in taking risks	This is a combination of the Anglo-Saxon runes 'Peorth', the dice cup, mysteries, secrets, chances and gambles, and 'Jear', prosperity, a fruitful harvest.
	Success in speaking and writing	This is a combination of several versions of the 'Ansuz' rune in different forms, overlapped, side by side, reinforcing the rune's meaning of divine communication with 'Æsir', the principal pantheon of the Norse gods.
	Victory	This is a combination of two overlapping 'Tiwaz' runes, the Norse warrior god 'Tyr', justice and victory, and may also be said to contain overlapping 'Ansuz', divine communication, and 'Æsir', the principal pantheon of the Norse gods.

Magical Symbolism 2. Bindrunes

Symbol	Name	Meaning
	Triumph	This is a combination of three overlapping 'Tiwaz' runes, the Norse warrior god 'Tyr', justice and victory, and may also be said to contain overlapping 'Ansuz', divine communication, and 'Æsir', the principal pantheon of the Norse gods.
	Success	This is a combination of 'Berkano', growth, rebirth, new beginnings, bringing things into being, and 'Jera', prosperity, a fruitful harvest, natural harmony of magical will.
	Safe journey	This is a combination of 'Raido', the chariot, travel, evolution, riding, a spiritual journey, and 'Algiz', protection, a shield, warding off evil, a guardian spirit, spiritual cleansing, travelling through other worlds.
	Safe journey	This is a combination of 'Ehwaz', a horse, transportation, change, physical travel, and 'Algiz', protection, a shield, warding off evil, a guardian spirit, spiritual cleansing, travelling through other worlds.
	Safe journey	This is a combination of 'Ehwaz', a horse, transportation, change, physical travel, and 'Algiz', protection, a shield, a guardian spirit, travelling through other worlds, and 'Uruz', speed, strength, and untamed potential.

Symbol	Name	Meaning
	Safe journey	This is a combination of 'Raido', the chariot, travel, evolution, riding, a spiritual journey, and 'Uruz', speed, strength, and untamed potential.
	Financial windfall	This is a combination of the Anglo-Saxon run 'Stan' meaning stone, stability, and 'Haegl', completeness and bringing into being.
	Personal financial security	This is a combination of two 'Algiz' runes overlapped, protection, security, a shield, and 'Fehu', wealth, abundance, moveable wealth, riches.
	Prosperity	This is a combination of 'Fehu', wealth, abundance, moveable wealth, riches, and 'Nauthiz', wants and needs, binding to oneself.
	Prosperity	This is a combination of 'Ingwaz', internal growth, storing or transferring magical power, 'Fehu', wealth, abundance, luck, energy, prosperity, cattle, moveable wealth, and two overlapping 'Algiz', protection, a shield, warding off evil.

3. Bindrunes for Norse Deities

Symbol	Name	Meaning
	Baldr	God, braveness, boldness, defiance, heroism,
	Bil	Goddess, immediacy, following the moon across the heavens, agriculture
	Bragi	God, poetry, music, wisdom, persuasive speech
	Dellingr	God, the dawn
	Eir	Goddess or Valkyrie, health, healing, medical skill
	Forseti	God, justice, reconciliation, mediation.
	Freyja	Goddess, love, beauty, fertility, sex, war, gold, seiðr, magic
	Freyr	God, sacred kingship, virility, peace and prosperity, sunshine, fair weather, good harvest

Magical Symbolism   *3. Bindrunes for Norse Deities*

Symbol	Name	Meaning
	Frigg	Goddess, foresight, wisdom
	Fulla	Goddess, bounty, plenty, healing
	Gefjon	Goddess, ploughing, harvest, foreknowledge
	Gerðr	Goddess, earth, fertility, gardens, fertile earth
	Gersemi	Goddess, beauty, fertility
	Gná	Goddess, divine messenger, fullness
	Gullveig	Goddess, rebirth, magic,
	Gungnir	The spear of Odin, the swaying one

Symbol	Name	Meaning
	Heimdallr	God, watchfulness, keen senses, foreknowledge, sight, hearing
	Hermóðr	God, divine messenger, bravery
	Hlín	Goddess, protection, refuge, peace and quiet, help, salvation, rescue
	Hnoss	Goddess, beauty
	Höðr	God, warrior, brave in battle, blind strength
	Hœnir	God, creation, reason, indecision, survival
	Iðunn	Goddess, eternal youth, fertility, apples
	Ilmr	Goddess, scent, fate, fertility, protective spirit
	Irpa	Goddess, fortune, luck, victory
	Ítreksjóð	God, travel, youth
	Kvasir	God, wisdom, travel, knowledge, poetry

Magical Symbolism   3. Bindrunes for Norse Deities

Symbol	Name	Meaning
	Lóðurr	God, creation, growth
	Lofn	Goddess, comfort, love, gentle manner, marriage
	Loki	God, Trickery, deception, shape-shifting
	Magni	God, might
	Máni	God, the moon, travelling through the heavens
	Meili	God, travel
	Mímir	God, knowledge, wisdom, secret knowledge, divine counsel
	Móði	God, wrath
	Nanna	Goddess, joy, peace, the moon
	Nerthus	Goddess, fertility

Magical Symbolism   3. Bindrunes for Norse Deities

Symbol	Name	Meaning
	Njörðr	God, the sea, seafaring, wind, fishing, wealth, crop fertility
	Njörun	Goddess, the earth
	Nordic Money Talisman	
	Óðinn	God, wisdom, healing, death, royalty, the gallows, knowledge, war, battle, victory, sorcery, poetry, frenzy, the runic alphabet, leader of the possessed.
		A variation of this 'Othala' rune (left) has been depicted as an astrological symbol for Asteroid #3989 known as 'Odin' discovered on 8th September 1986 by P Jensen at the Brorfelde Observatory in Denmark. The name and number of this asteroid was allocated by the Minor Planet Center (MPC) which is part of the Smithsonian Astrophysical Observatory.
	Óðr	God, divine madness, frantic, fury, vehemence, eagerness, the mind, feeling, song, poetry, frenzy
	Rán	Goddess, the sea

Magical Symbolism   *3. Bindrunes for Norse Deities*

Symbol	Name	Meaning
	Rindr	Goddess, vengeance
	Sága	Goddess, foretelling the future
	Sif	Goddess, the earth, wheat, fertility, family, marriage
	Sigyn	Goddess, victory
	Sister-wife of Njörðr	Goddess, fertility
	Sjöfn	Goddess, love, marriage, relationships
	Skadi	Goddess, bow hunting, skiing, winter, mountains, snow, ice
	Skuld	Goddess, that which should be
	Snotra	Goddess, wisdom
	Sól	Goddess, the sun
	Syn	Goddess, defence, refusal

Symbol	Name	Meaning
	Þorgerðr Hölgabrúðr	Goddess, fortune, luck, victory
	Þórr	God, lightning, thunder, storms, sacred groves and trees, strength, hallowing, fertility
	Þrúðr	Goddess, strength
	Tyr	God, war, justice, divine judgment, sacrifice
	Ullr	God, archery, glory
	Urðr	Goddess, fate, that which will be
	Váli	God, vengeance, survival
	Valkyrie	Goddesses, fate, battle, the afterlife
	Vár	Goddess, oaths, agreements, pledges
	Verðandi	Goddess, happening, present, that which is

Magical Symbolism   3. *Bindrunes for Norse Deities*

Symbol	Name	Meaning
	Vé	God, priest, holy, sanctuary, idol, temple
	Víðarr	God, wide-ruling, vengeance, survival
	Vili	God, will, wish, determination
	Vör	Goddess, carefulness, awareness, wisdom
	Web of Urdr	The well of fate, destiny

4. Staves and Symmetry

Using symmetry in a stave is a way of increasing the meaning and significance of the stave. You can either repeat the same symbol many times, many variations of the same symbol, or many different symbols of your choosing that combine together to form a constellation of meaning. The possibilities are potentially infinite.

Isaz staves

In this example, the simplest rune, Isaz, is drawn in increasing levels of symmetry, compounding and amplifying its meaning, which could be strengthening concentration and will, maintaining something as it is, binding, holding on to something, halting movement.

Ansuz staves

In this example, the rune Ansuz is drawn in the same way, symbolising magical incantation, convincing and magnetic speech, gaining wisdom, and divine communication, finding the truth in the matter, increasing magical energies

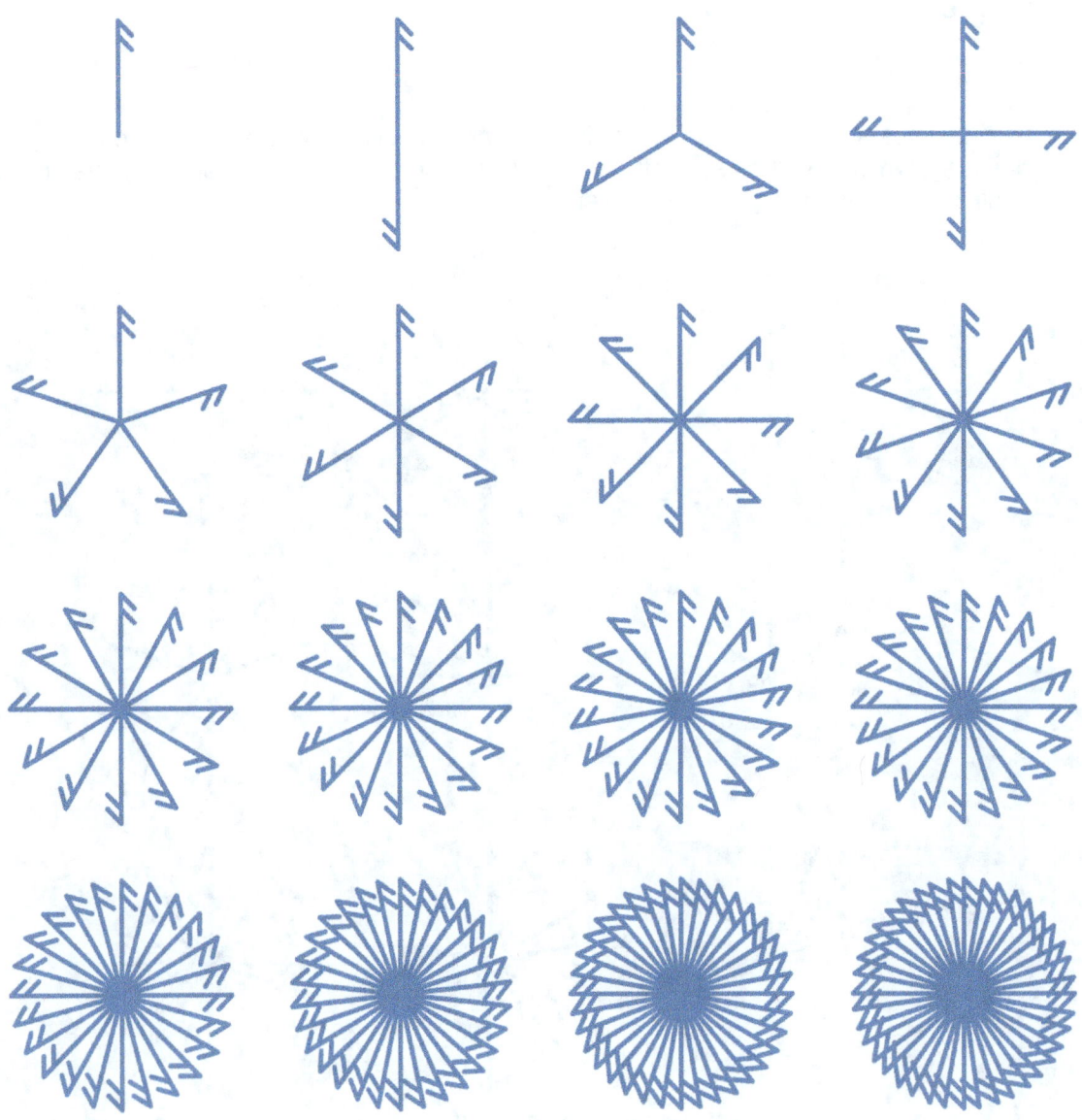

5. Galdrastafir

Galdrastafir are a uniquely Icelandic continuation of the tradition of magical symbols in the Norse world, which appear to have evolved stylistically from ever more complex bindrunes into staves, widening to incorporate other elements, such as 'stave modifiers' which appear similar to runes from later runic alphabets, but serving the function of catching, trapping, amplifying, or rerouting the energy within the stave, configured in many different combinations of symmetrical, asymmetrical, and polygonal designs. Preserved in manuscripts from the Late Middle Ages until the 20th Century, they also incorporate references to biblical seals and elements of the Christian faith. The relationship between traditional magic and religious symbolism is a complex and varied one.

Protection

Against All Witchery

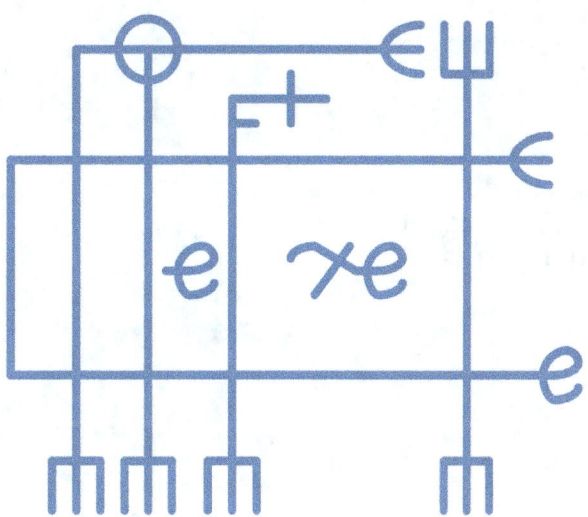

Against Foreboding When You
Go Into Darkness

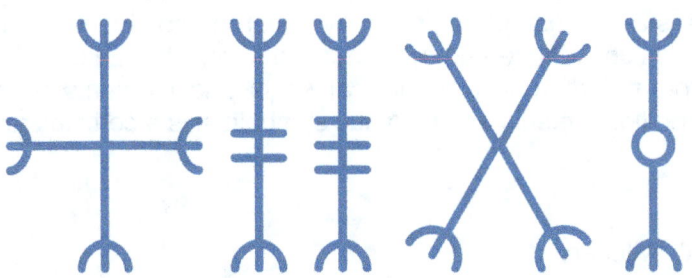

Fransskriftarstafur 1
(French-Script Stave Against
Hatred and Evil Thoughts 1)

Magical Symbolism 5. *Galdrastafir*

Fransskriftarstafur 2
(French-Script Stave Against
Hatred and Evil Thoughts 2)

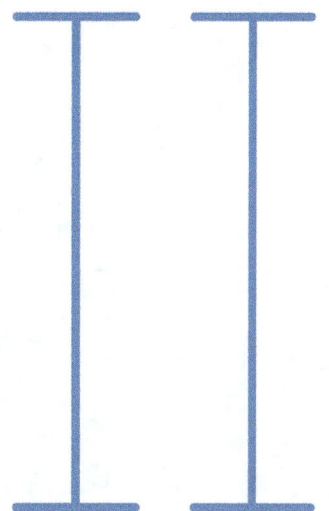

Fransskriftarstafur 3
(French-Script Stave Against
Hatred and Evil Thoughts 3)

Magical Symbolism 5. Galdrastafir

Herzlustafir
(Strengthening Staves)
IB 383 4to 0027r 01
LBS 2917a 4to 0015v 02
LBS 4627 8vo 0014r 01

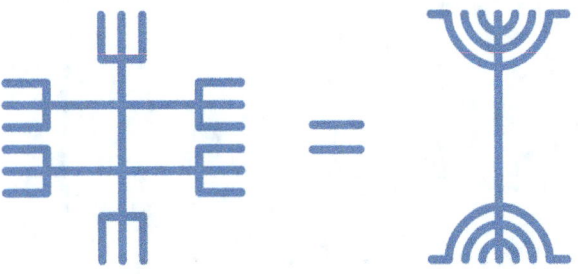

Hjálmur
(Helm)
LBS 4375 8vo 0023v 04

You will never go insane.

Innsigli Salomons 1
(Seal Of Solomon 1)
IB 383 4to 0025v 01
LBS 2917a 4to 0013r 01

Lukkuhringur
(Luck Ring)

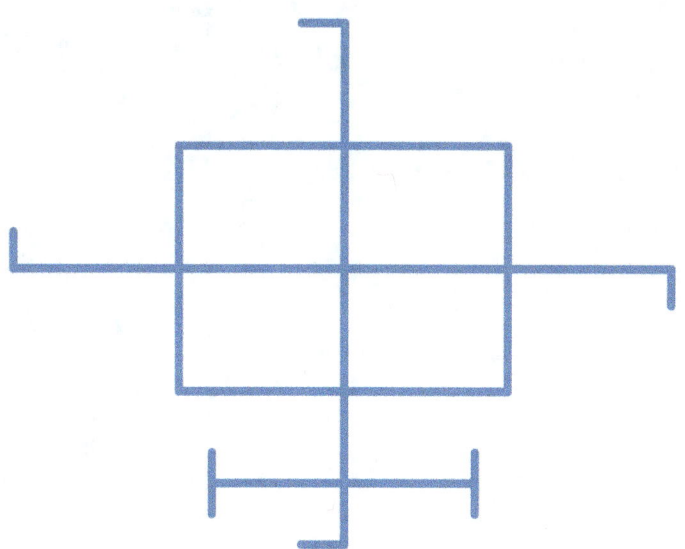

Lífsstafur
(Life Stave)
LBS 4375 8vo 0026v 01

Máni
(Moon)
LBS 4375 8vo 0023v 05

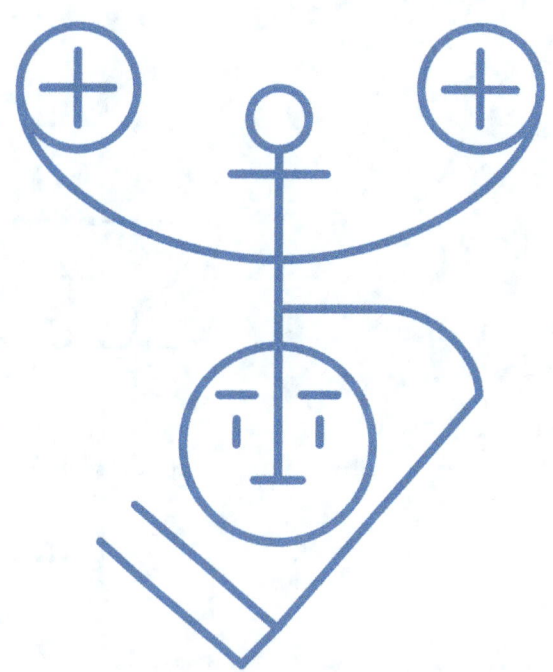

Protection
LBS 2413 8vo 0035r 02

Protection Against Sorcery

Magical Symbolism   *5. Galdrastafir*

Return To Sender

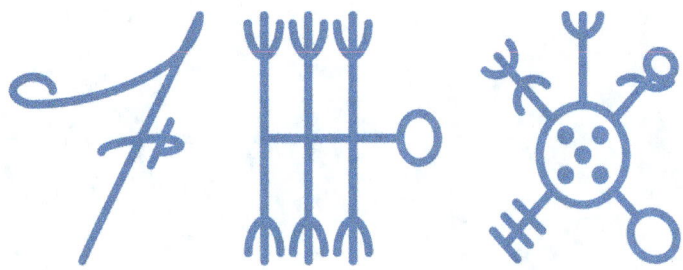

Rosahringur Minni
(Lesser Circle Of Protection)
LBS 4375 8vo 0014r 01

Signetshringur
(Signet Ring)

Smjörhnútur
(Butter Knot)

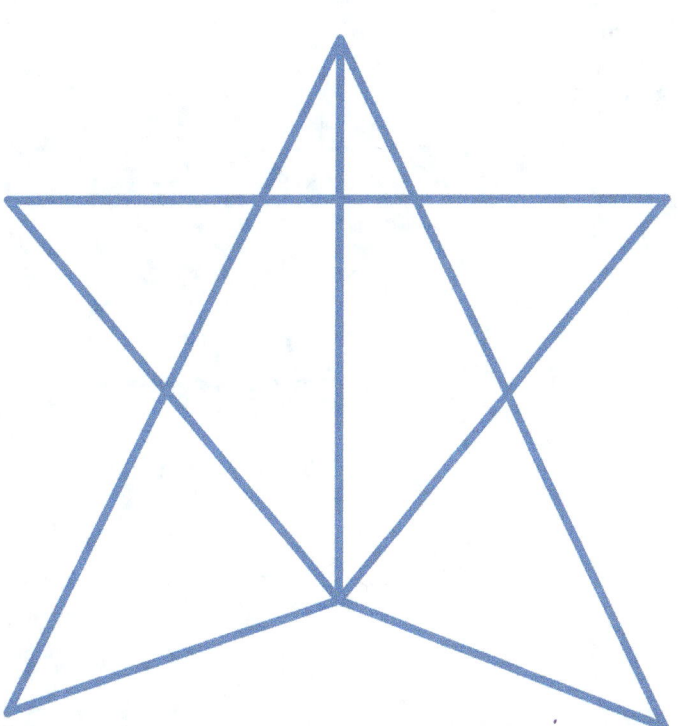

Magical Symbolism 5. Galdrastafir

Sól
(Sun)
LBS 4375 8vo 0023v 06

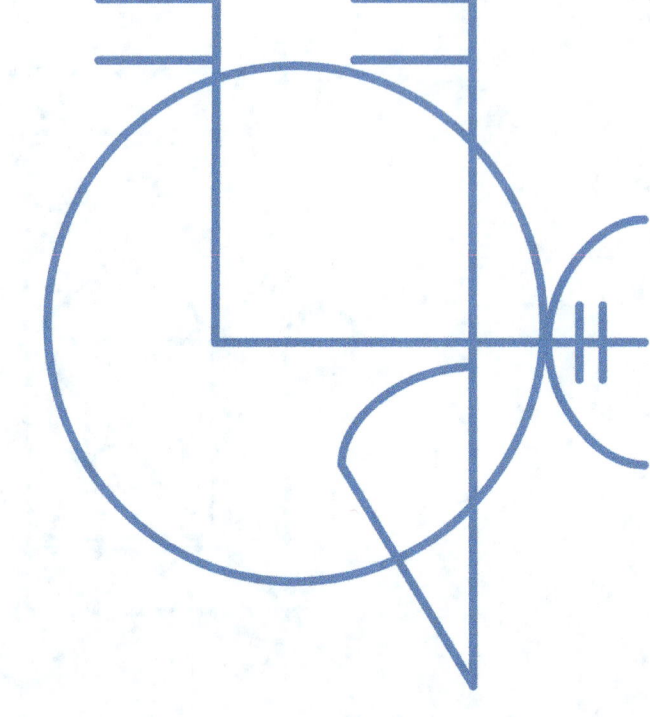

Sorcery Prevention
LBS 2413 8vo 0011r 02
LBS 2413 8vo 0031r 02

Magical Symbolism 5. *Galdrastafir*

Stafir Gegn Galdri
(Staves Against Witchcraft)
LBS 143 8vo 0012v 01

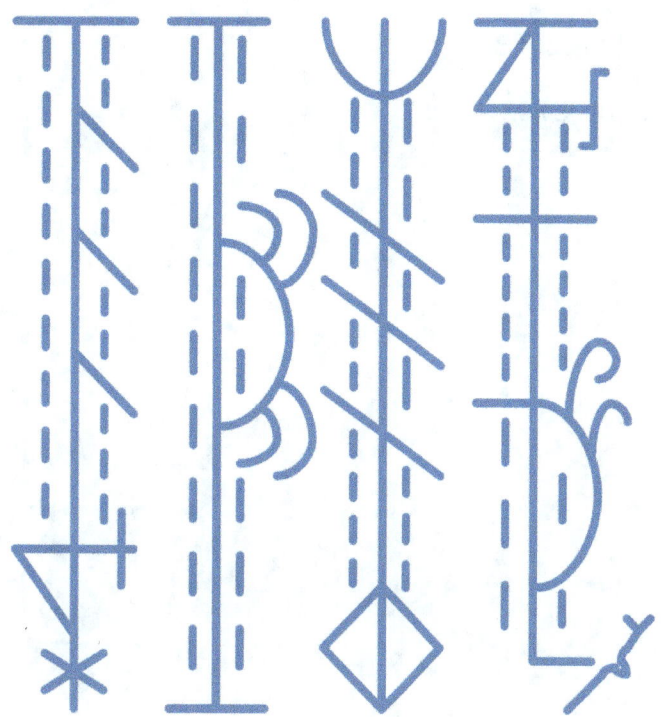

Stafur Mót Aðsókn Anda 1
(Stave Against Attacks By Spirits 1)
LBS 4375 8vo 0005v 01

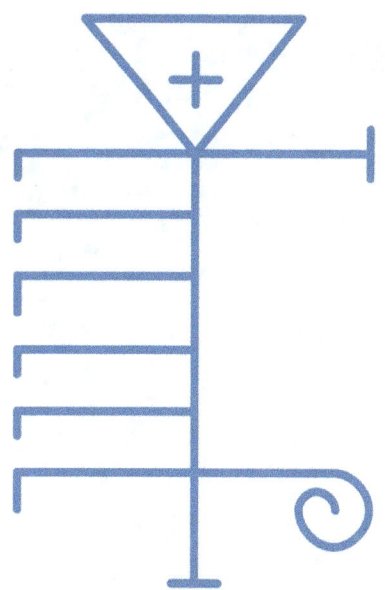

46

Stafur Mót Adsokn Anda 2
(Stave Against Attacks By Spirits 2)
LBS 4375 8vo 0005v 02

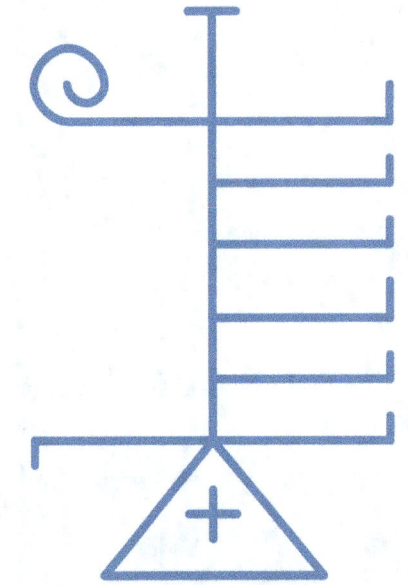

Stafur Mót Adsokn Anda 3
(Stave Against Attacks By Spirits 3)
LBS 4375 8vo 0005v 03

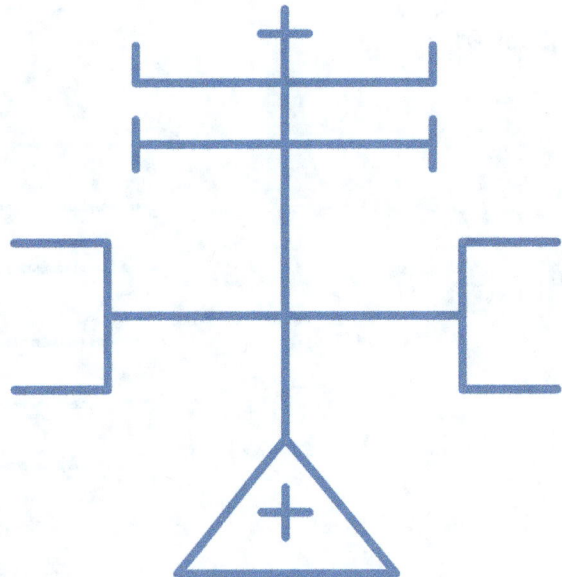

Stafur Til Að Varna Galdri 1
(Stave To Defend Against
Sorcery 1)
LBS 2917a 4to 0017r 01
LBS 4627 8vo 0018v 01
LBS 977 4to 0046v 06

Stafur Til Að Varna Galdri 2
(Stave To Defend Against
Sorcery 2)
LBS 2917a 4to 0025r 02

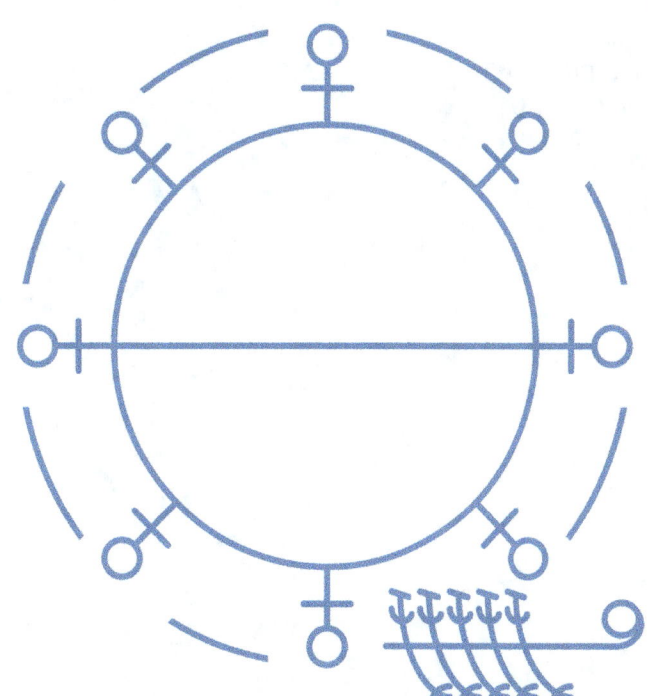

Magical Symbolism 5. Galdrastafir

Sverð
(Sword)
LBS 4375 8vo 0023v 01

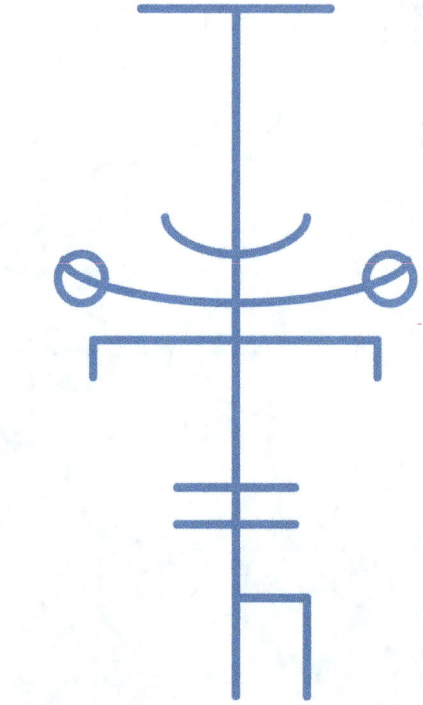

Þórshamar
(Thor's Hammer)
LBS 2917a 4to 0020v 03
LBS 4375 8vo 0010r 01

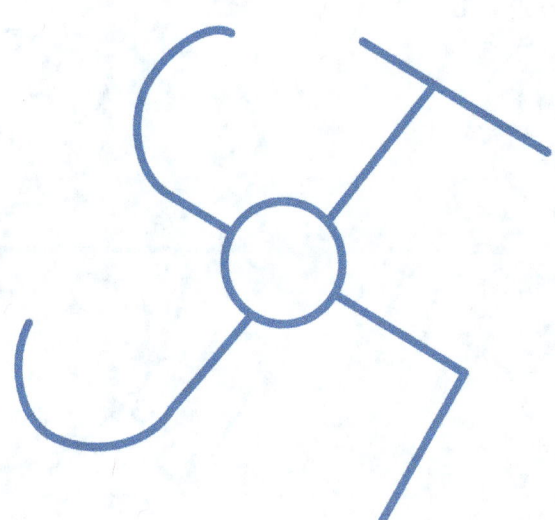

Varnarrósin
(Rose Of Protection)

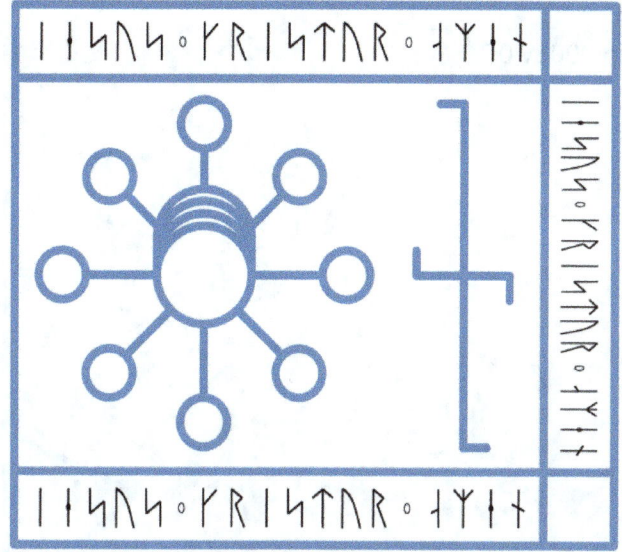

Varnarstafur Mót Illum Öndum 1
(Stave Of Protection Against Evil Spirits 1)
LBS 2413 8vo 0030r 01
LBS 2413 8vo 0031v 05
LBS 4375 8vo 0008v 04
LBS 4689 8vo 0010v 01
LBS 977 4to 0033v 06
LBS 977 4to 0040v 13

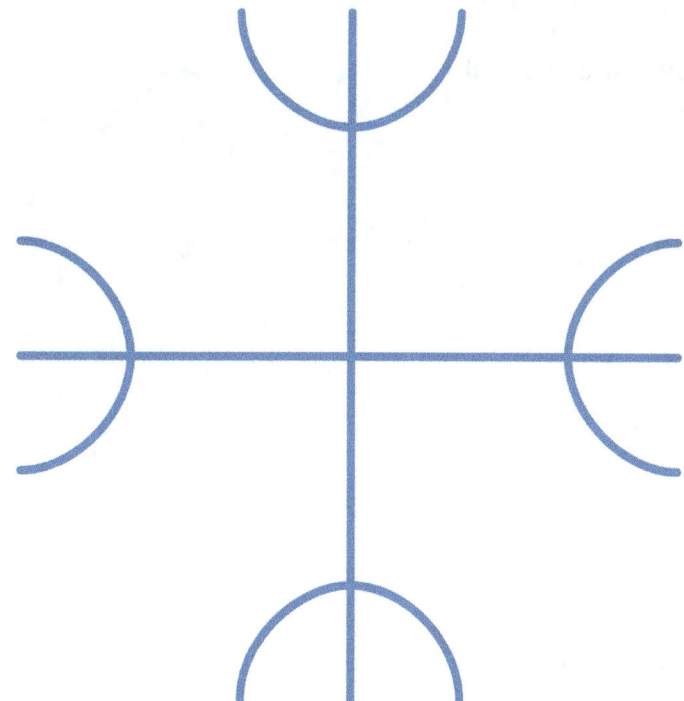

Varnarstafur Mót Illum Öndum 2
(Stave Of Protection Against Evil Spirits 2)
LBS 4375 8vo 0008v 05

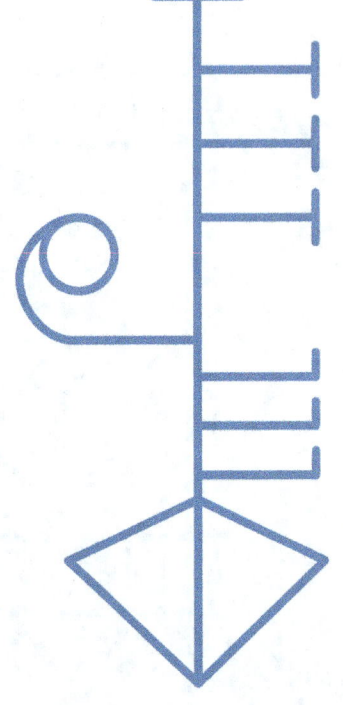

Varnarstafur Mót Illum Öndum 3
(Stave Of Protection Against Evil Spirits 3)

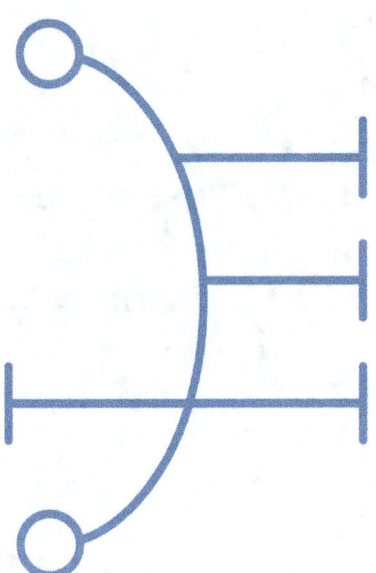

Vegvísir
(Waymark)
IB 383 4to 0026v 01
LBS 2917a 4to 0015r 01
LBS 4627 8vo 0017v 01

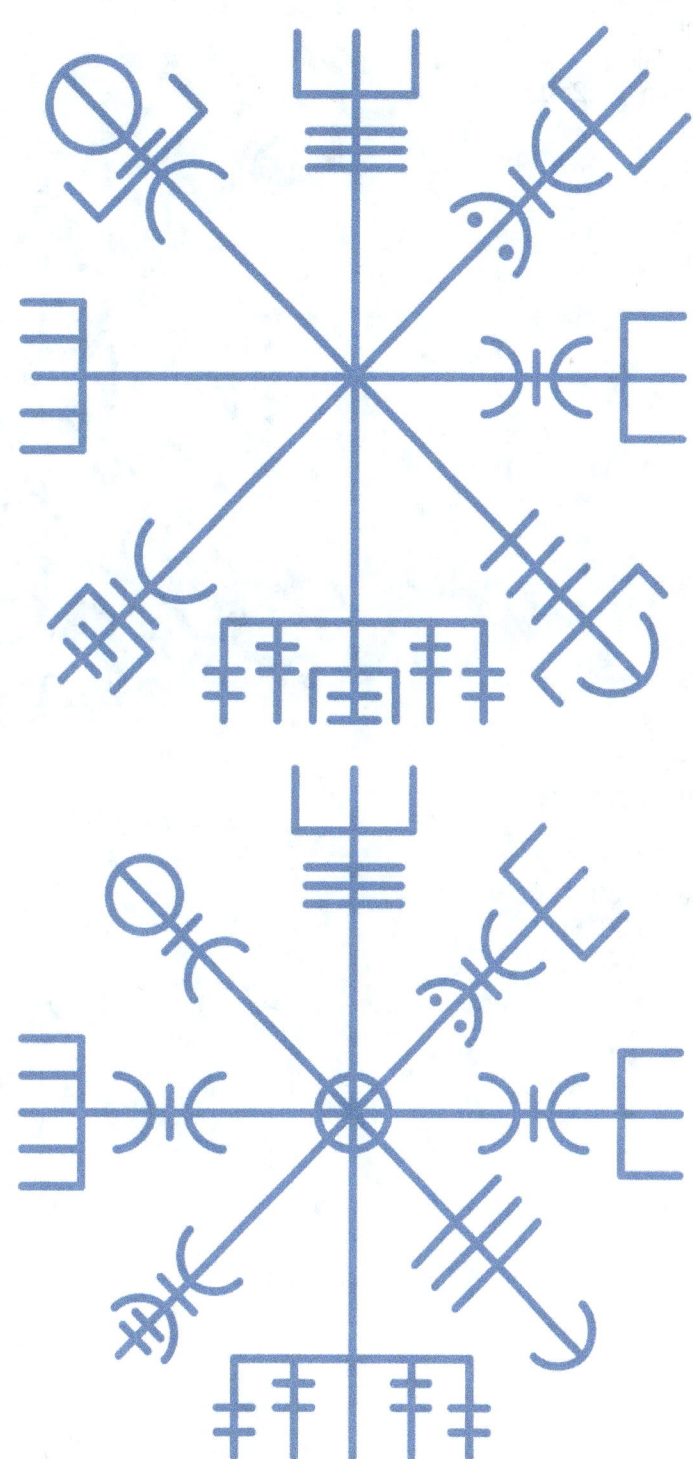

Magical Symbolism 5. *Galdrastafir*

Veldismagn
(Power Amplifier)
LBS 4375 8vo 0022r 02

Vörn Gegn Hatri
(Protection Against Hatred,
Reconciler)
IB 383 4to 0025v 04
LBS 2917a 4to 0014r 02
LBS 4689 8vo 0018v 03
LBS 977 4to 0044v 01

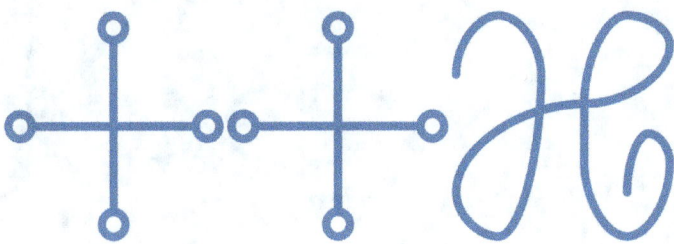

Love

Að Ná Ástum Kvenna
(To Win The Love Of A
Woman)
LBS 2917a 4to 0023r 02

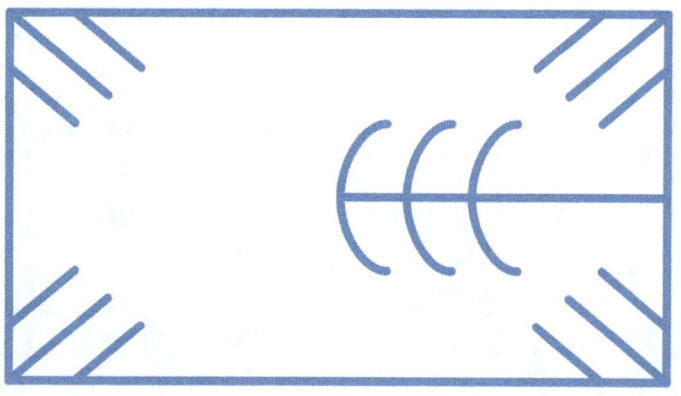

Að Ná Ástum Kvenna
(To Win The Love Of A
Woman)

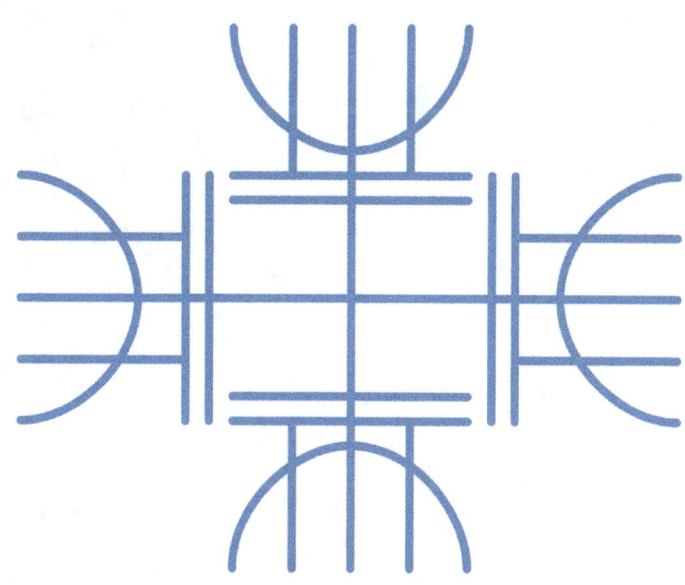

Að Unni
(To Win a Girl's Heart)
LBS 4375 8vo 0032r 01

Stafur Til Að Fá Stulku
(Stave To Win A Girl's Heart)
LBS 4375 8vo 0004v 02

Galdur Fái Maður Aðsvif Eða
Faraldur 1
(To Win A Girl's Love 1)
ATA Amb 2 F 16-26
LBS 2413 8vo 0013v 05
LBS 2413 8vo 0031v 03

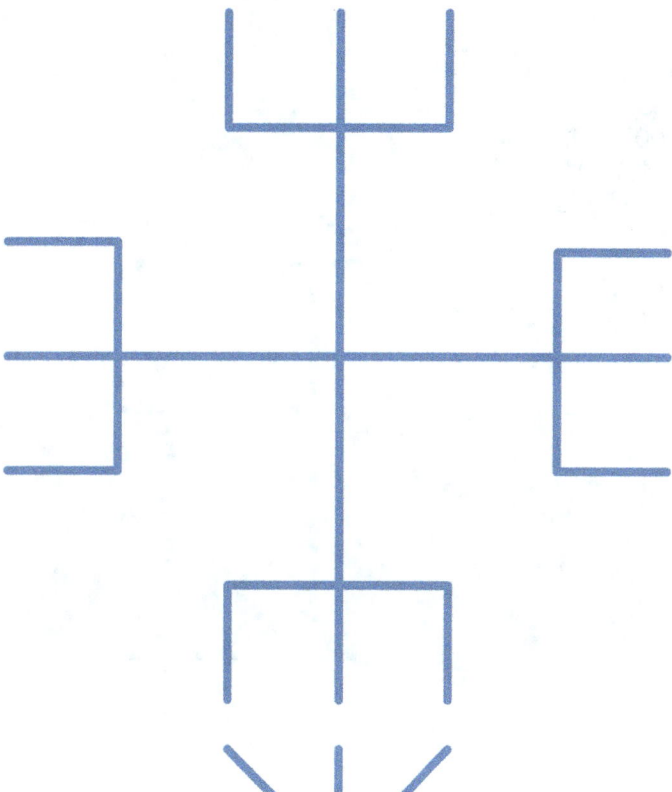

Galdur Fái Maður Aðsvif Eða
Faraldur 2
(To Win A Girl's Love 2)
ATA Amb 2 F 16-26

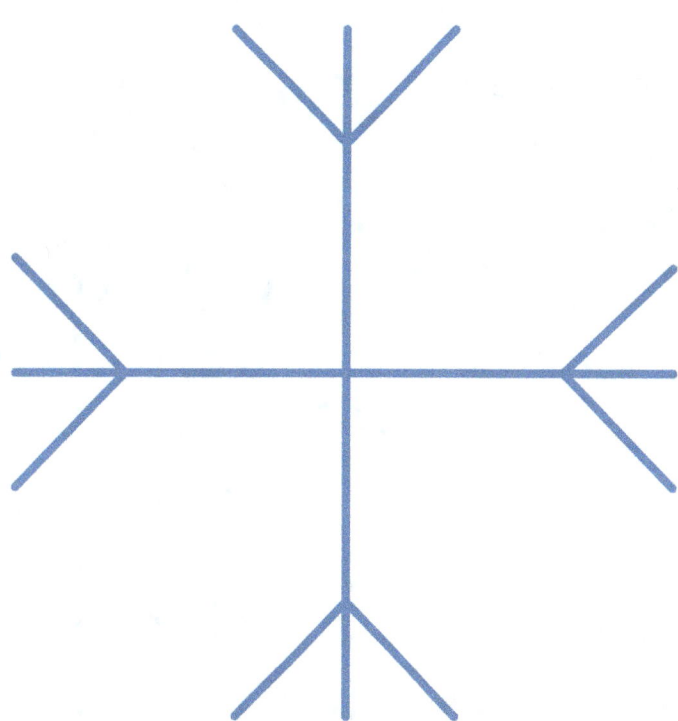

Magical Symbolism 5. Galdrastafir

Luck

Lukkustafir
(Luck Staves)
IB 383 4to 0024r 03
LBS 2917a 4to 0010v 02
LBS 4627 8vo 0018r 03

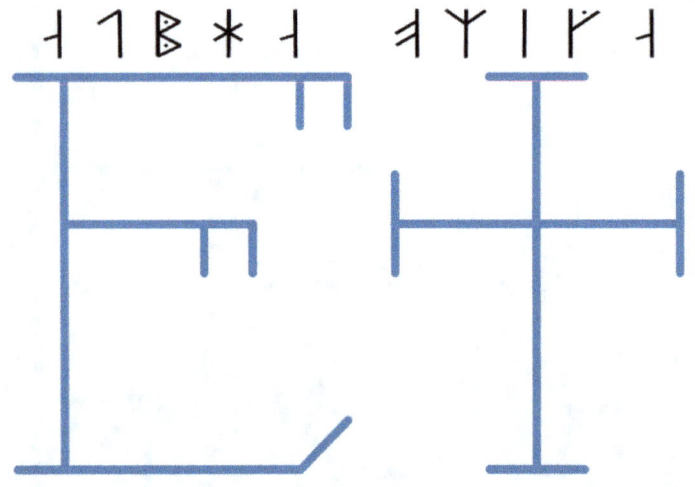

Heillahnútur (The Good Luck Knot)
LBS 2413 8vo 0037v 01

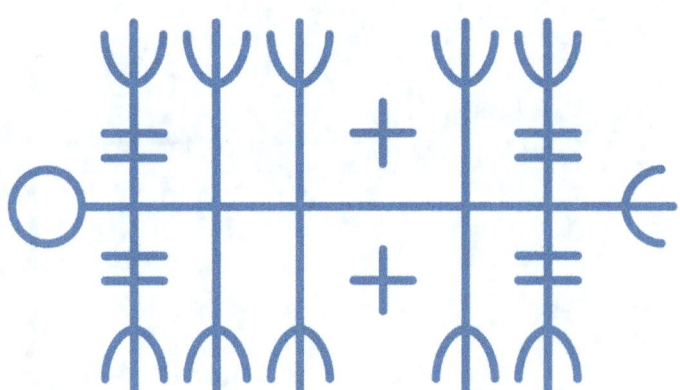

Magical Symbolism 5. Galdrastafir

Enhancement

Discovering The Unknown
LBS 2413 8vo 0028r 04

Setting Intentions

Bænarstafur
(Prayer or Wishing Stave)

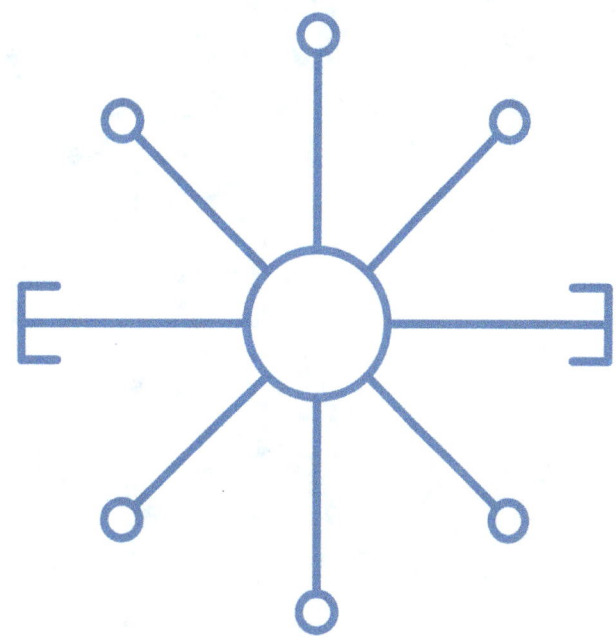

Feingur
(A fertility rune)
IB 383 4to 0024v 03
LBS 2917a 4to 0012r 02
LBS 4627 8vo 0019r 01

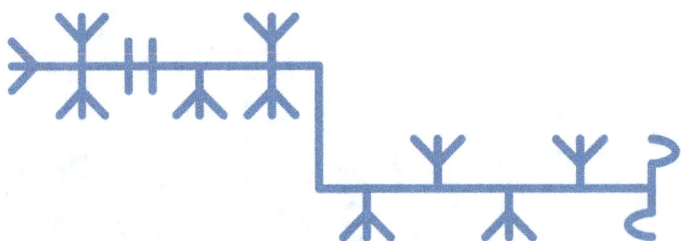

Hjálparhringir Karlamagnúsar
(Charlemagne's Rings of Assistance)
LBS 143 8vo 0008v 01
LBS 143 8vo 0009r 01
LBS 143 8vo 0009v 01
LBS 2917a 4to 0036v 01
LBS 4375 8vo 0006r 01

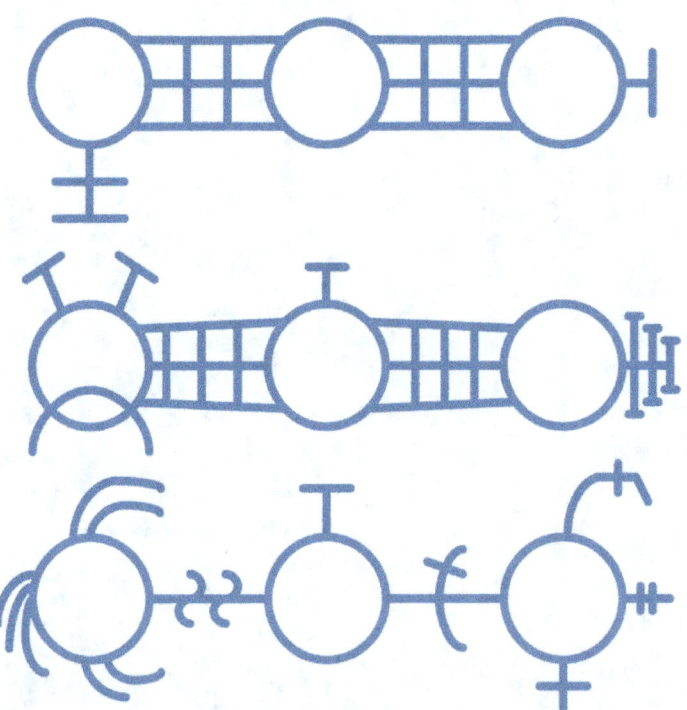

Kaupaloki 1
(Deal Closer 1)
IB 383 4to 0023r 01
LBS 2917a 4to 0009r 01
LBS 4627 8vo 0013v 01

Kaupaloki 2
(Deal Closer 2)
IB 383 4to 0023r 03
LBS 2917a 4to 0009v 01
LBS 4627 8vo 0013v 02

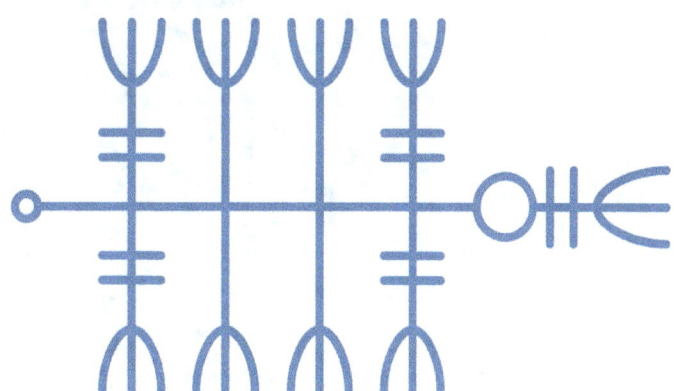

Kaupaloki 3
(Deal Closer 3)
LBS 2917a 4to 0020r 01
LBS 4375 8vo 0009v 07
LBS 4627 8vo 0010r 02

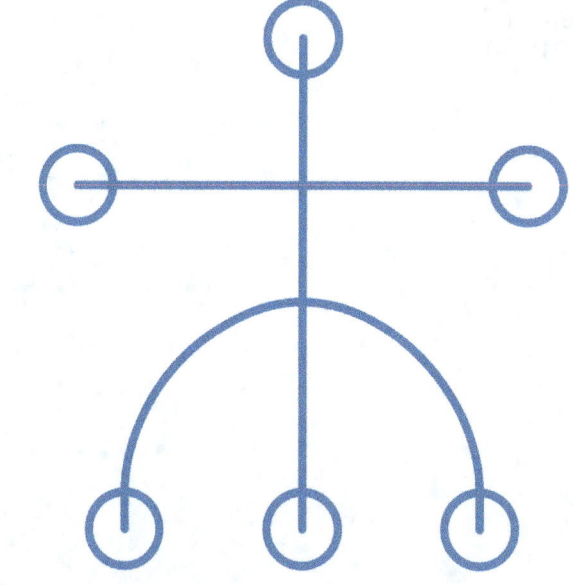

Sigurmerki
(Victory Sign)
LBS 2917a 4to 0017v 01

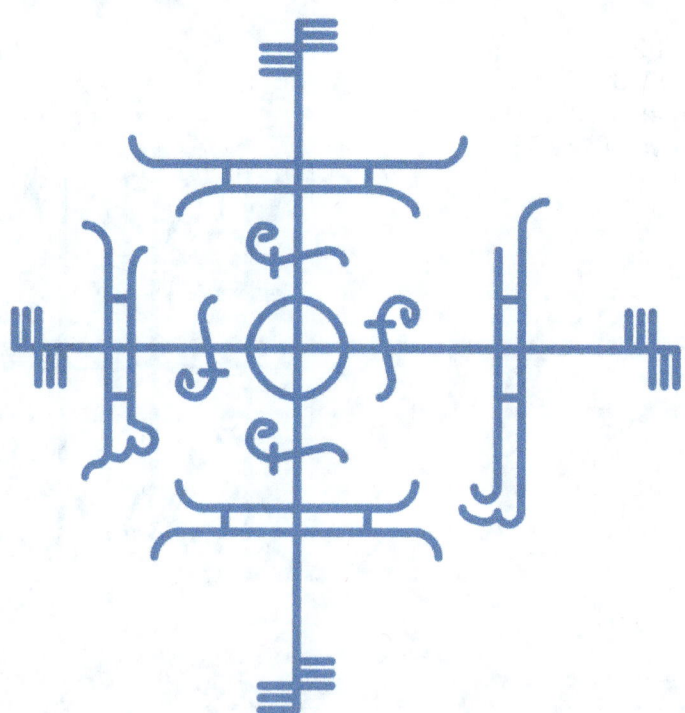

Success
LBS 2917a 4to 0021r 03

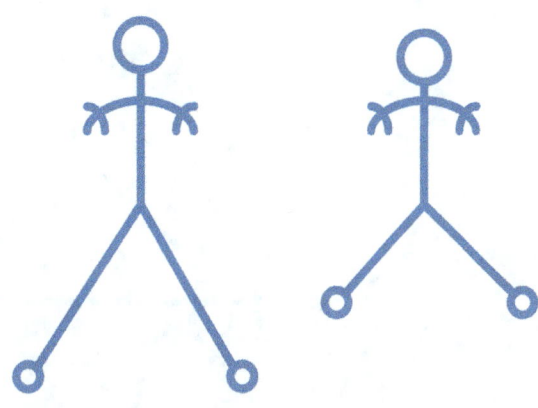

To Acquire The Object You
Crave
LBS 2413 8vo 0010v 01
LBS 4689 8vo 0017r 02
LBS 977 4to 0038v 01

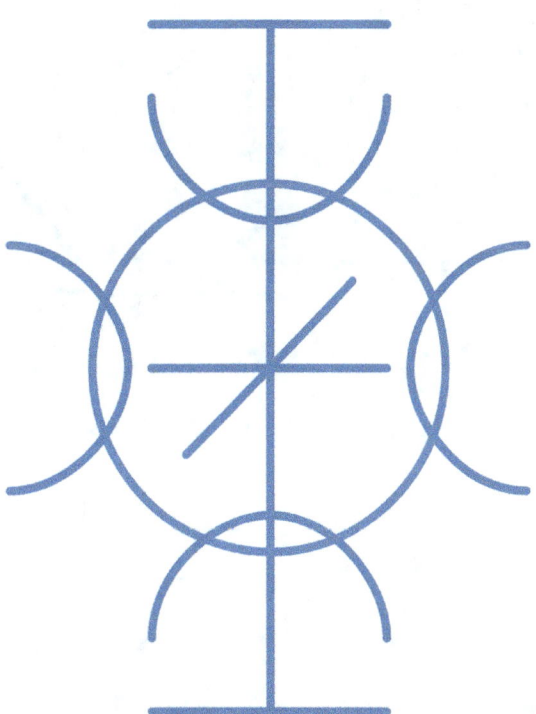

To Get Your Own Wish
LBS 2413 8vo 0008v 02

To Have Success In Business
LBS 2413 8vo 0009v 02

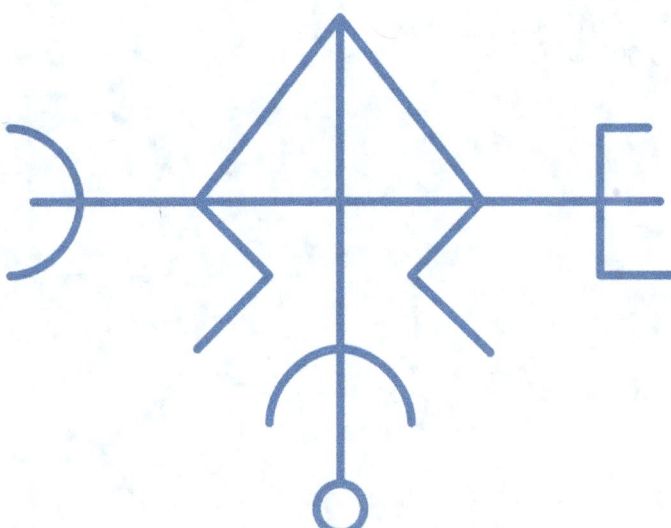

To Overcome Enemies

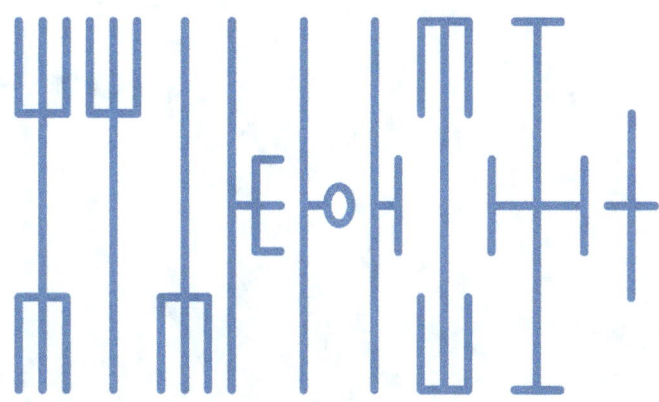

Umbótarstafur
(Stave Of Ameliorations)
LBS 2917a 4to 0022v 01

Magical Symbolism   5. *Galdrastafir*

Victory In Business With All People

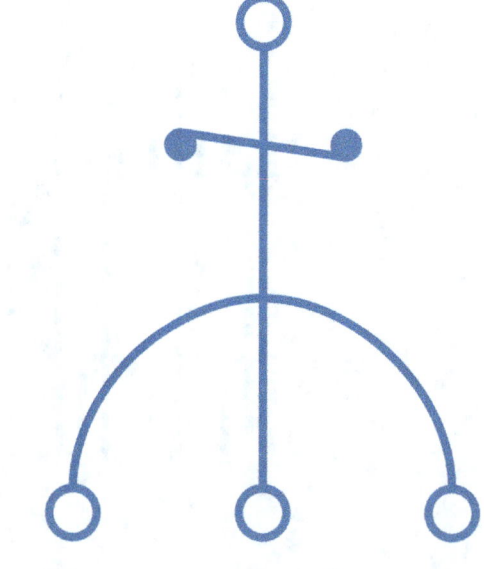

Victory

Magical Symbolism 5. Galdrastafir

Sleep & Dreams

Against Sleeplessness And
Bad Dreams

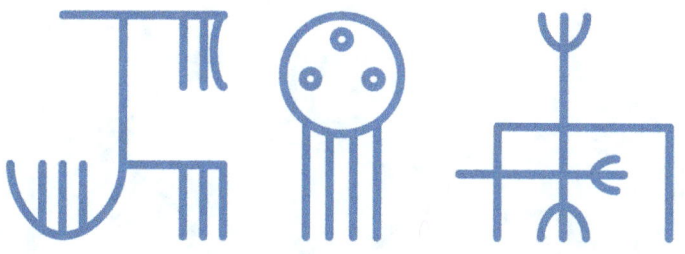

Draumstafir Hinir Mestu
(Greatest Dream Staves)
IB 383 4to 0024r 01
LBS 2917a 4to 0011r 01
LBS 4627 8vo accMat08v 03

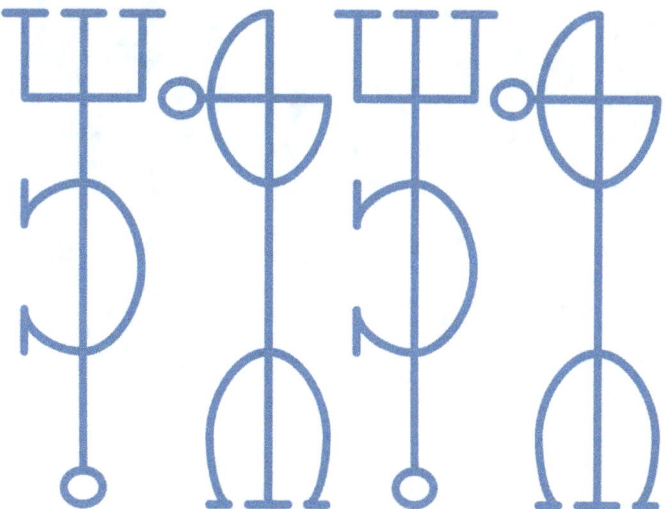

Draumstafur
(Dream Stave)
LBS 4375 8vo 0001r 01

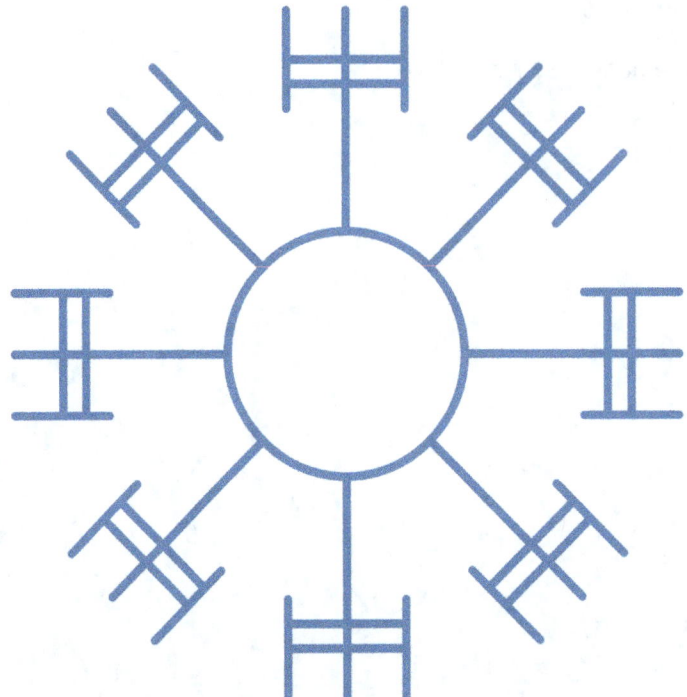

Draumstafur Hinn Meiri
(Greater Dream Stave)
IB 383 4to 0023v 02
LBS 2917a 4to 0010r 01
LBS 4627 8vo accMat08v 02

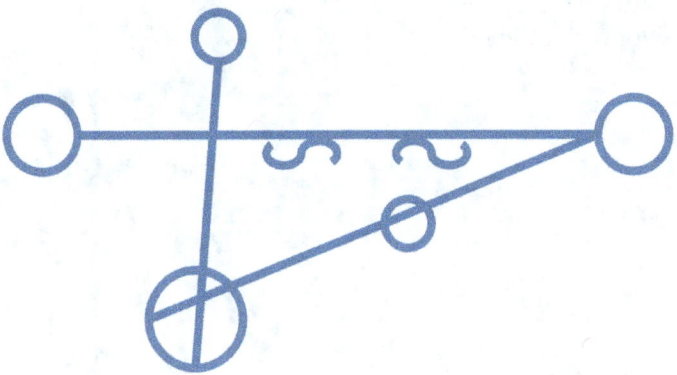

Magical Symbolism 5. *Galdrastafir*

Draumstafur Hinn Minna
(Lesser Dream Stave)
IB 383 4to 0023v 03
LBS 2917a 4to 0010r 02

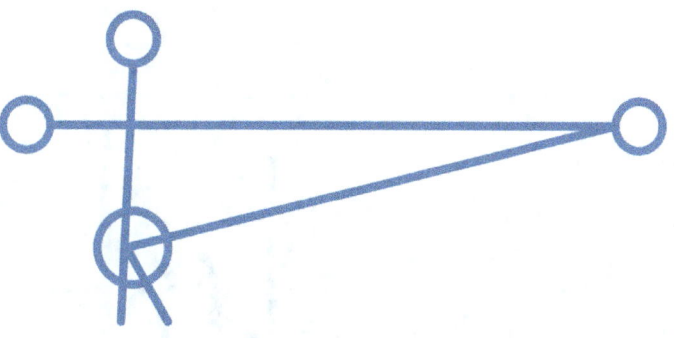

Magical Symbolism 5. *Galdrastafir*

Svefnþorn
(Sleep-Thorn)
IB 383 4to 0024r 02
LBS 2917a 4to 0010v 01

Magical Symbolism 5. *Galdrastafir*

Svefnþorn 2
(Sleep-Thorn 2)
LBS 4375 8vo 0001v 04

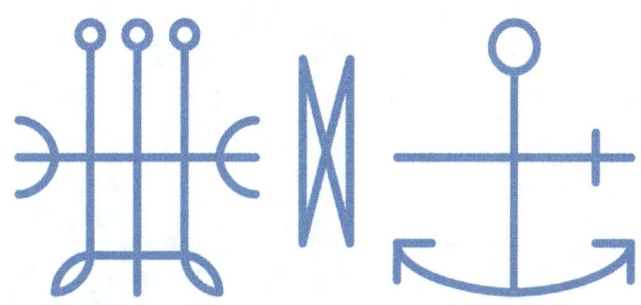

Galdur Til Að Svæfa Mann
(To Make Someone Go To Sleep)

Magical Symbolism   5. Galdrastafir

Legal

Dunfaxi
(Down-Mane, To Win a Law Case)

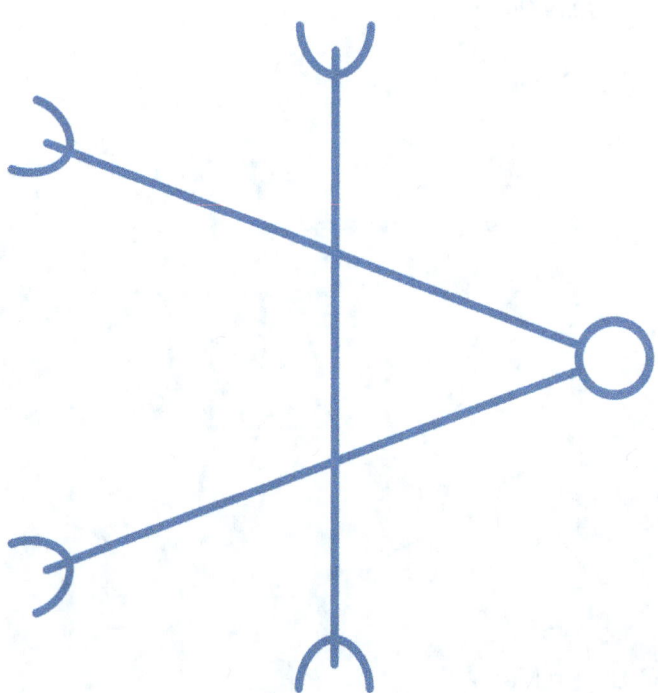

Magical Symbolism   5. *Galdrastafir*

Máladeilan, Máldeyfa
(To Win in Court)
LBS 4375 8vo 0001r 02

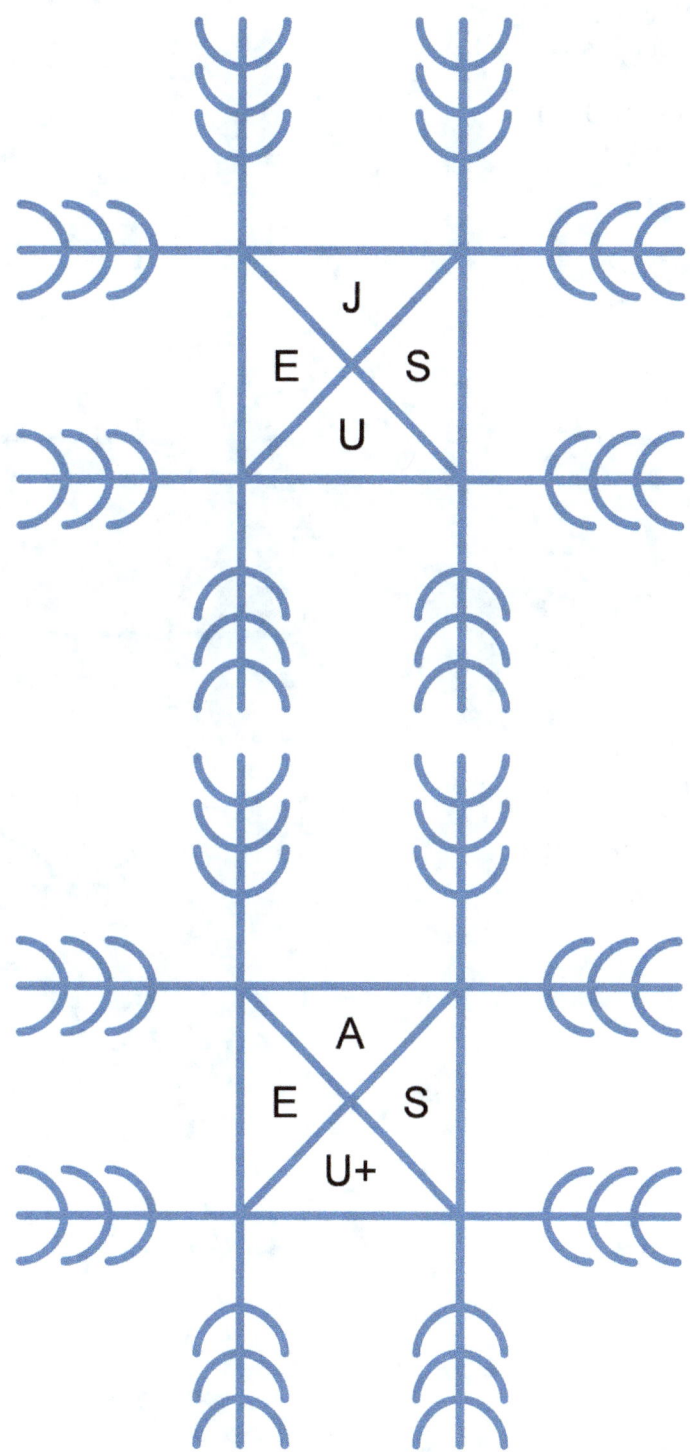

Stafur Til Málfylgju 1
(Stave For Support In Legal Cases 1)
LBS 4375 8vo 0002r 01

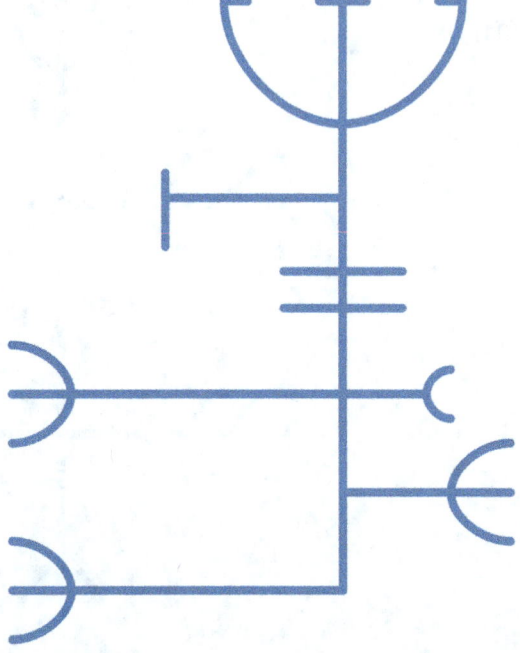

Stafur Til Málfylgju 2
(Stave For Support In Legal Cases 2)
LBS 4375 8vo 0002r 02

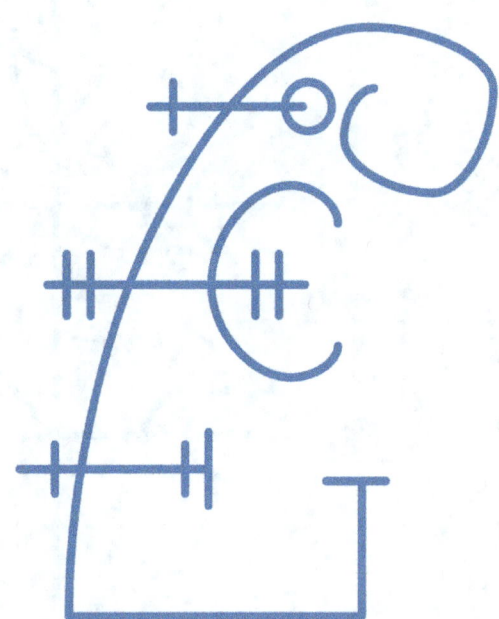

Influencing Behaviour

Berreininn, Þagnarstafur
(Bare Stallion, Stave Of Silence)
LBS 4375 8vo 0006r 02

Missýningastafurinn Óðinn
(Delusion Stave of Odin)

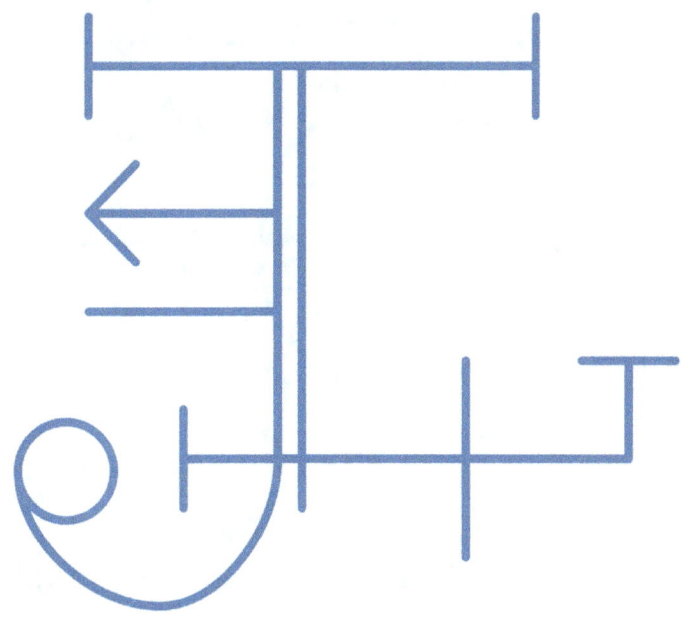

Magical Symbolism 5. Galdrastafir

The Silencer

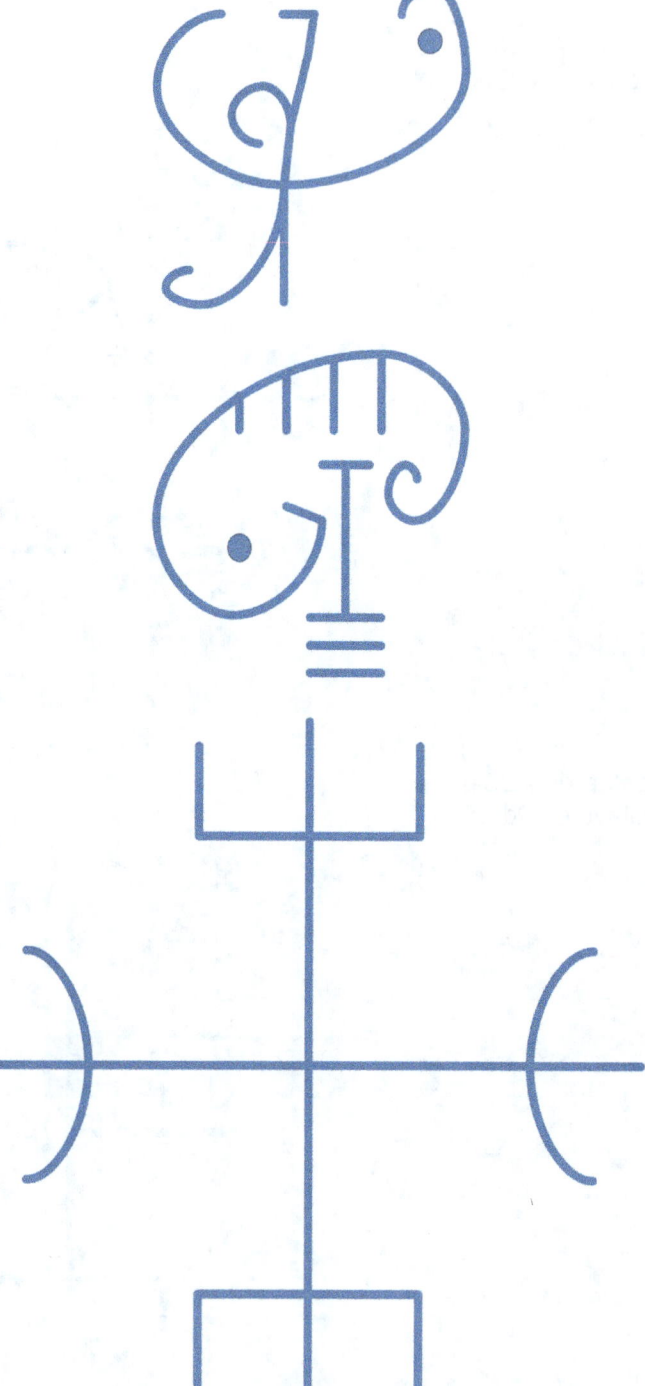

Galdur Til Að Stilla Alla Reiði
(To Calm Anger)
ATA Amb 2 F 16-26

Magical Symbolism 5. *Galdrastafir*

Concealment

Concealment
LBS 2413 8vo 0021r 04

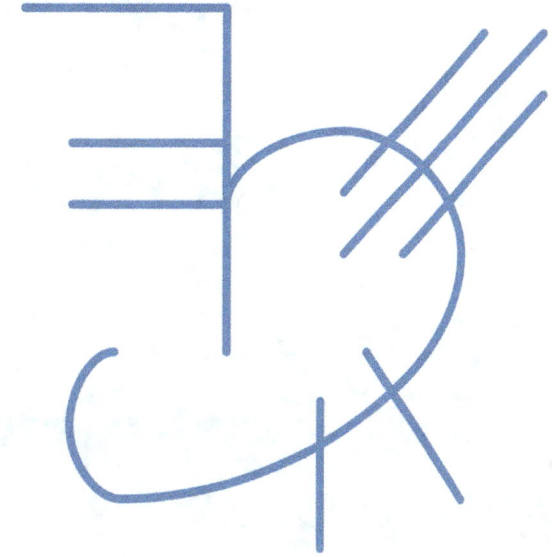

Hulinshjálmur
(Helm Of Concealment)
LBS 4375 8vo 0011v 01
LBS 4375 8vo 0020v 01

Hulinshringir
(Rings Of Concealment)
LBS 4375 8vo 0005r 02

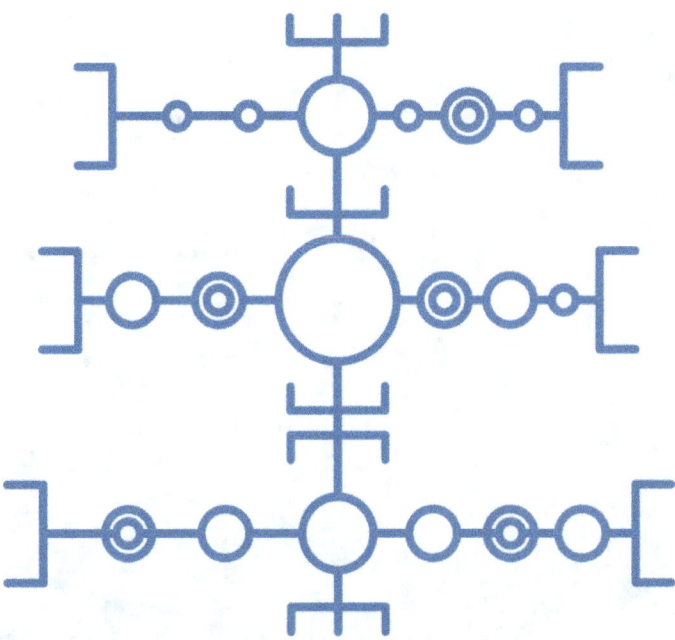

Strength in the face of enemies

Ægishjálmur 1
(Helm of Awe 1)

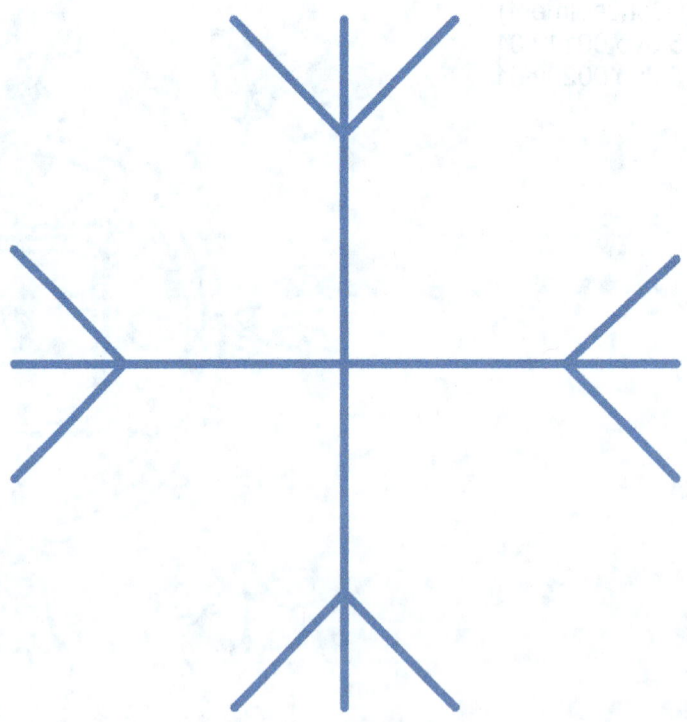

Magical Symbolism 5. *Galdrastafir*

Ægishjálmur 2
(Helm of Awe 2)

Ægishjálmur Hinn Gamli
(Helm of Awe the Elder)
LBS 143 8vo 0011r 01
LBS 2917a 4to 0037v 01
LBS 4375 8vo 0001v 01

Skelkunarstafur, Óttastafur
(Fear Stave)
IB 383 4to 0024r 04
LBS 2917a 4to 0011r 02
LBS 4627 8vo 9999r-RB 02

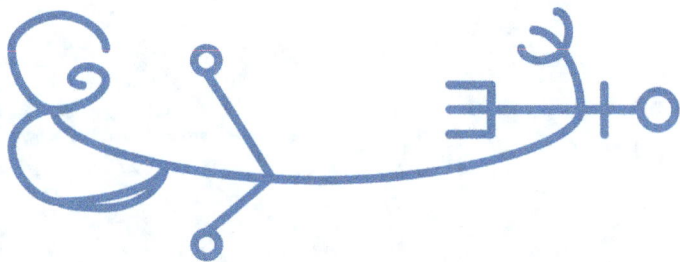

Hræðigaldur
To Cause Fear In An Enemy
ATA Amb 2 F 16-26

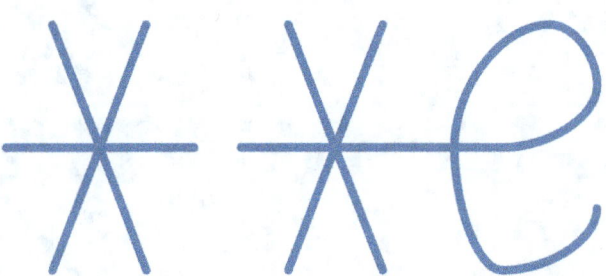

Magical Symbolism 5. *Galdrastafir*

Árásargaldur
(To Cause Fear In Your Enemies)

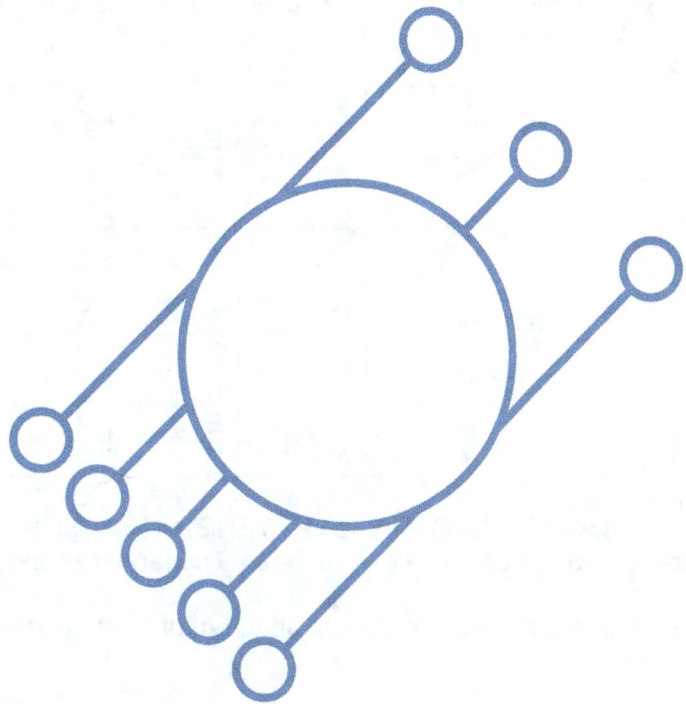

Against Enemies

Stafur Mót Óvin Þínum
(Stave Against Your Enemy)
LBS 4375 8vo 0001v 03

Magical Symbolism   5. Galdrastafir

The name 'Rotas Cross' is from the magic table called the 'Sator Square' or 'Rotas Square' which contains a series of 5 letter words in Latin.

S	A	T	O	R
A	R	E	P	O
T	E	N	E	T
O	P	E	R	A
R	O	T	A	S

R	O	T	A	S
O	P	E	R	A
T	E	N	E	T
A	R	E	P	O
S	A	T	O	R

SATOR = The sower, AREPO = (A name), TENET = Holds, OPERA = Work, ROTAS = Turning. Roughly translated this could be said to mean 'The farmer Arepo holds the work of turning the plough'.

The letters when rearranged are also an anagram of 'Pater Noster', the first two words of the Lord's Prayer in Latin.

				P				
				A				
				T				
		A		E		O		
				R				
P	A	T	E	R	N	O	S	T	E	R
				O				
		O		S		A		
				T				
				E				
				R				

Rotas crosses have a talismanic protective quality. The more that are used, the more effective they are.

Rotaskross 01
(Rotas Cross 01)

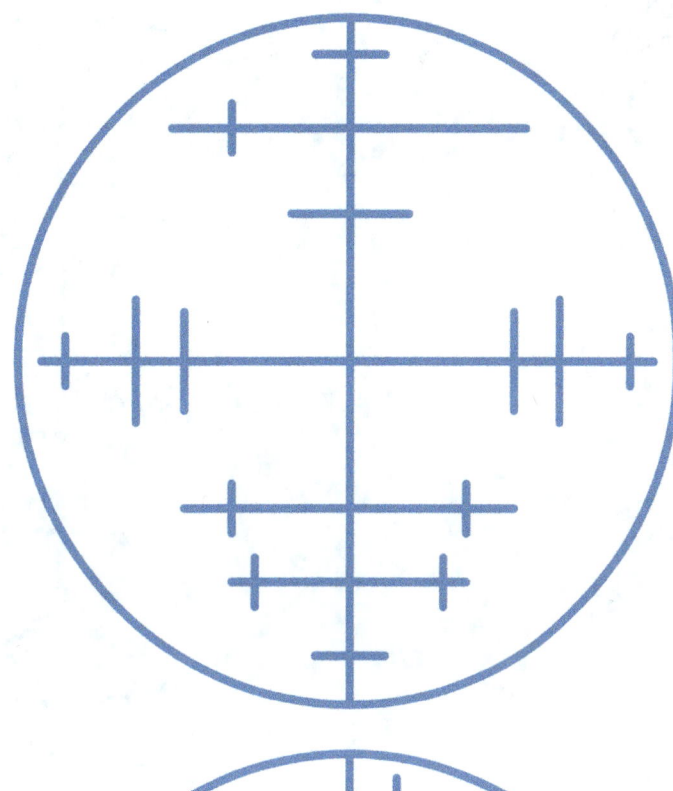

Rotaskross 02
(Rotas Cross 02)

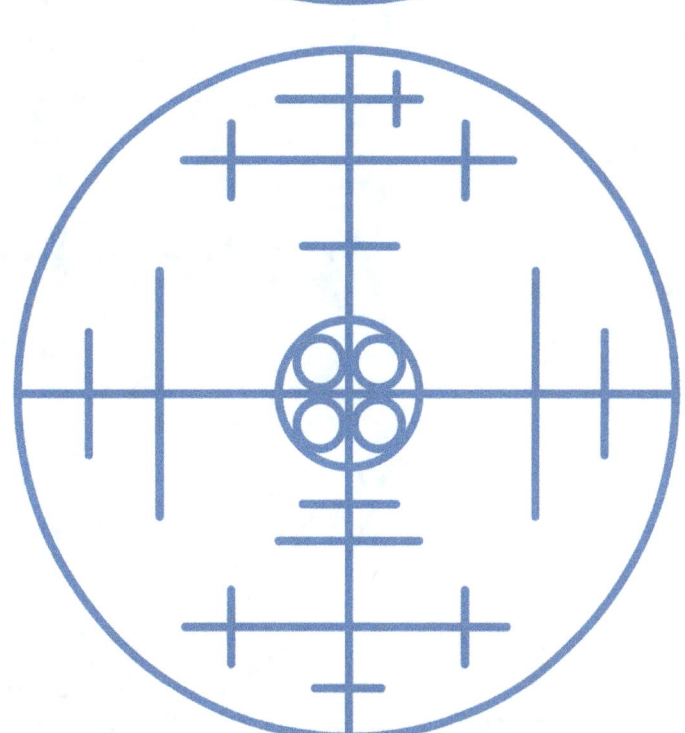

Rotaskross 03
(Rotas Cross 03)

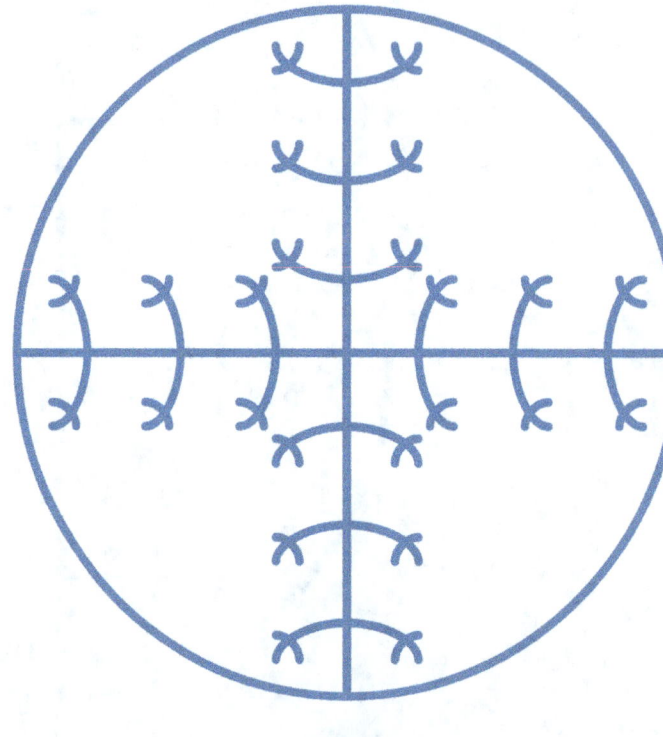

Rotaskross 04
(Rotas Cross 04)

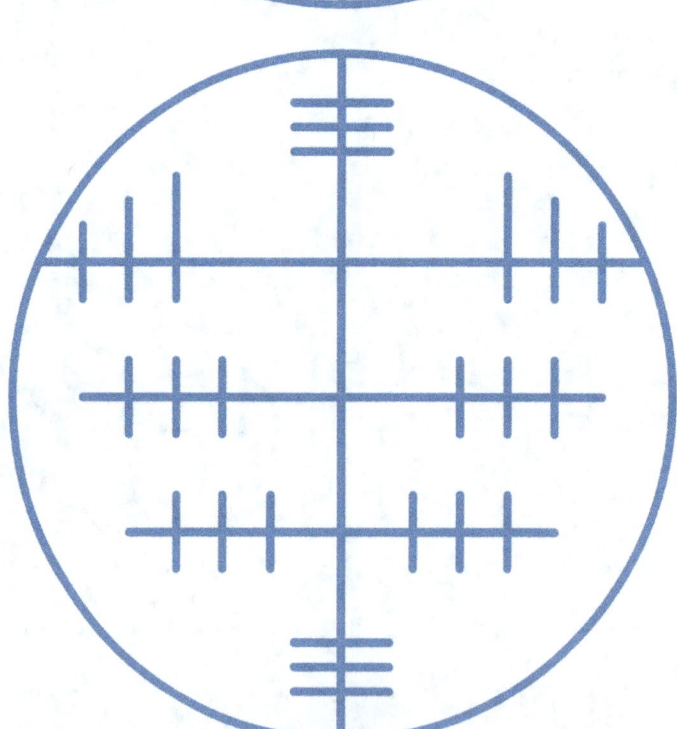

Magical Symbolism 5. *Galdrastafir*

Rotaskross 05
(Rotas Cross 05)

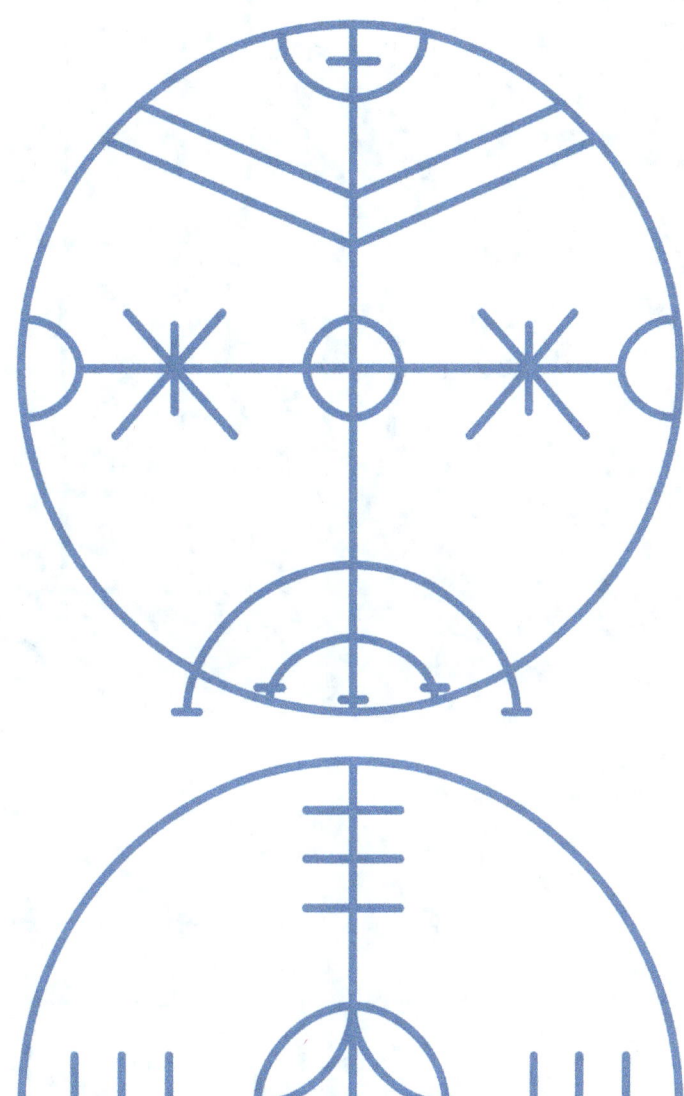

Rotaskross 06
(Rotas Cross 06)

Rotaskross 07
(Rotas Cross 07)

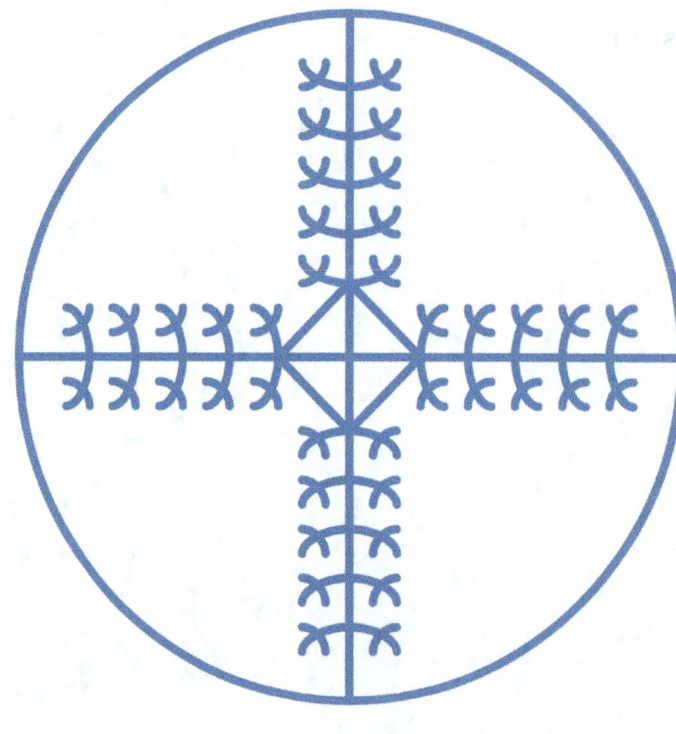

Rotaskross 08
(Rotas Cross 08)

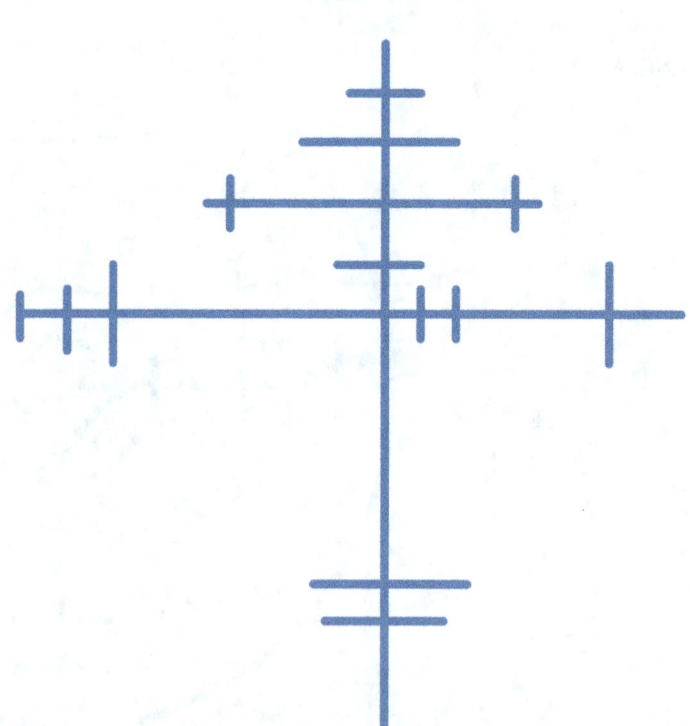

Magical Symbolism   *5. Galdrastafir*

Rotaskross 09
(Rotas Cross 09)
LBS 977 4to 0034r 04
LBS 4375 8vo 0001v 02
LBS 4375 8vo 0003v 02

Rotaskross 10
(Rotas Cross 10)
LBS 2917a 4to 0033r 01

Rotaskross Eiriks Jarls
(Lesser Rotas Cross Of Earl Eirikur)

Rotaskross Olafs Konungs
(Rotas Cross Of The King Olafur)
IB 383 4to 0026r 02

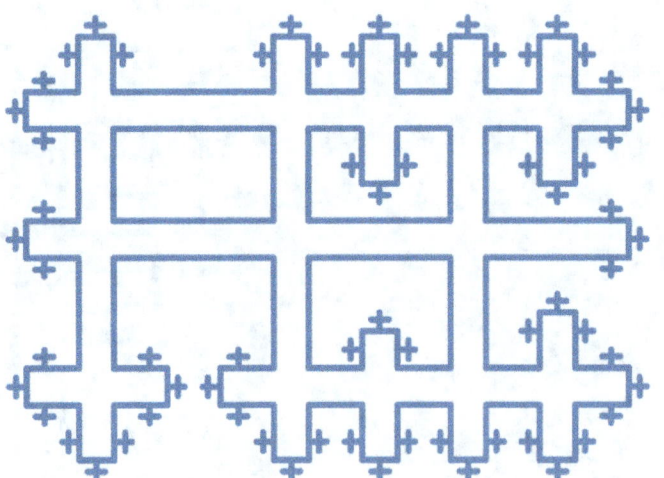

Rotaskross Stefnis
(Stefnir's Rotas Cross)

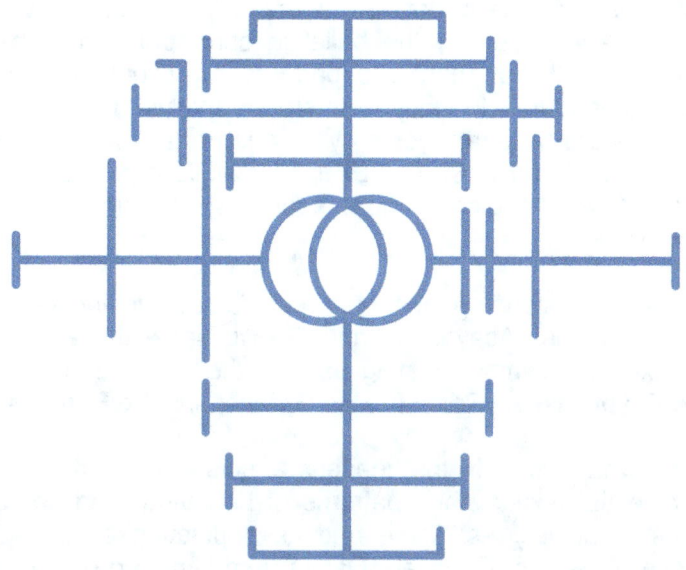

Rothukross
(Crucifix)
IB 383 4to 0026r 01
LBS 2917a 4to 0014v 01

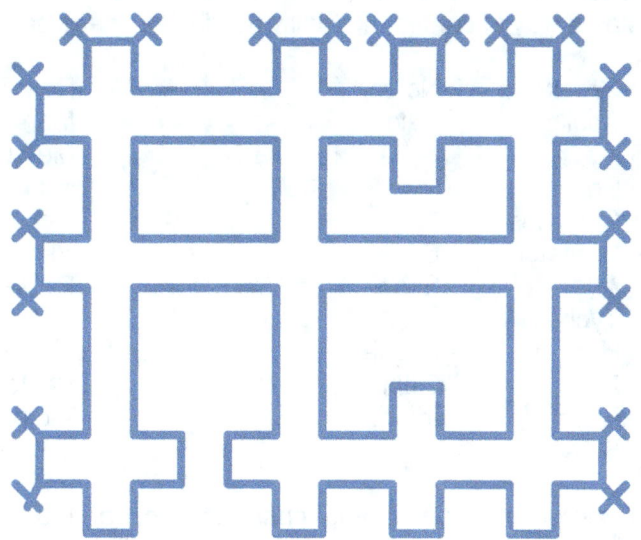

6. Astrological Symbols

Astrology is a systemic interpretation of mankind's relationship with the earth and the cosmos. This relationship is characterised by the belief in correspondences between celestial observations and terrestrial events, and that there are patterns representing divine communications which can be observed, categorised, catalogued, understood, and used to predict future events. Evidence of early human beings recording lunar cycles by means of carvings on bones goes back 25,000 years, and between 4000 B.C.E and 2500 B.C.E. the Neolithic agricultural revolution brought about a greater understanding of the changing of the seasons, which could be predicted by the rising and falling of different constellations.

Over time, the understanding of these celestial events increased in sophistication, and from the Sumerians, Akkadians, Assyrians, and Babylonians there is scattered evidence of copies of astrological texts with symbols dating back to the 3rd millennium B.C.E, which would later go on to influence the Egyptians, the Persians, the Greeks, and the Romans.

The belief that what occurs in the heavens affects events on earth lends itself to a synergy between the idea of celestial bodies, their patterns of behaviour and characteristics, and the behaviour and characteristics of deities. As Rome and its population expanded, so did its pantheon of deities, including those of Sabine, Etruscan, Oscan, and Umbrian origin, several of which were the same or similar to their Roman or Greek counterparts or equivalents, but with different spellings.

The discourse known as '*Interpretatio Graeca*' (Greek translation) was used in the Roman world to compare the characteristics, names, and origins of deities from Greek culture using similarities in characteristics as a way of confirming their own deities as the same, but with different names.

Roman	Greek	Norse	Roman	Greek	Norse
Apollo	Apollo	Baldr	Mars	Ares	Týr
Arcus	Iris		Mercury	Hermes	Hermóðr
Aurora	Eos		Minerva	Athena	Frigg, Freyja
Bacchus	Dionysus		Neptune	Poseidon	Njörðr
Ceres	Demeter	Sif	Pluto	Hades	Hel
Diana	Artemis	Skaði	Proserpina	Persephone	Ēostre
Fortuna	Tyche		Trivia	Hecate	
Juno	Hera	Frigga	Venus	Aphrodite	Freyja
Jupiter	Zeus	Óðinn	Vesta	Hestia	
Juventas	Hebe	Iðunn	Victoria	Nike	
Luna	Selene		Vulcan	Hephaestus	Þórr

These deities represent aspects and characteristics of mankind which have been externalised, personified, and mythologised as external forces which influence us at their whim. The worship, reverence, or appeasement of these deities is an attempt to either persuade them to look favourably upon us, or as a means of asking for protection or assistance in our lives and goals.

These symbols were preserved in manuscripts and codices in the Byzantine Empire, which then spread across Europe during the Renaissance, bringing about a revival of classical culture and the liberal arts, including astrology, which found its way into art in the form of allegorical paintings sketches, engravings, and also as symbols in the art of Alchemy, representing primes, elements, planetary metals, compounds, and processes.

Magical Symbolism   6. Astrological Symbols for Roman and Greek Deities

Symbol	Name	Meaning
	Apollo	God, oracles, healing, archery, music, the arts, sunlight, knowledge, youthfulness
	Arcus (Iris)	Goddess, rainbows, divine messenger
	Aurora (Eos)	Goddess, the dawn
	Bacchus (Dionysus)	God, wine, fertility, frivolity, ecstasy, theatre

Magical Symbolism 6. Astrological Symbols for Roman and Greek Deities

Symbol	Name	Meaning
	Bellona (Enyo)	Goddess, war, destruction, conquest
	Caelus (Uranus)	God, the sky, the heavens
	Calliope	Muse, eloquence, poetry
	Ceres (Demeter)	Goddess, harvest, agriculture, fertility, sacred law

91

Symbol	Name	Meaning
	Clio	Muse, history and legend, the lyre
	Concordia (Harmonia)	Goddess, concord, harmony
	Cupid (Eros)	God, desire, erotic love, attraction, affection
	Cybele (Magna Mater)	Goddess, the earth, the harvest, nature, protection
	Decima (Lachesis)	Goddess, fate, destiny, measurer of the thread of human life

Magical Symbolism   6. *Astrological Symbols for Roman and Greek Deities*

Symbol	Name	Meaning
	Deimos	God, dread, terror
	Diana (Artemis)	Goddess, hunting, the wilderness, the moon, chastity
	Dione	Goddess, healing

Magical Symbolism 6. Astrological Symbols for Roman and Greek Deities

Symbol	Name	Meaning
	Discordia (Eris)	Goddess, strife, discord
	Dysnomia	Goddess, lawlessness, chaos

94

Symbol	Name	Meaning
	Erato	Muse, love, love poetry
	Eunomia	Goddess, governance, law, legislation, order
	Euterpe	Goddess, music, lyric poetry
	Faunus (Pan)	God, nature, the wild, forests, plants, fields
	Felicitas	Goddess, happiness, blessing, luck, productivity, fertility

Symbol	Name	Meaning
	Fides	Goddess, trust, good faith, honour, credibility, fidelity, reliability, reciprocity
	Fortuna (Tyche)	Goddess, luck, fortune, prosperity, destiny
	Hyperion	God, father of the sun, the dawn, and the moon
	Iapetus	God, mankind, humanity

Magical Symbolism   6. Astrological Symbols for Roman and Greek Deities

Symbol	Name	Meaning
	Invidia (Nemesis)	Goddess, observer of justice being offended by undeserved success, divine retribution, punisher of arrogance before the gods
	Isis	Goddess, the afterlife, resurrection, marriage, protection of ships at sea, nature, the divine feminine
	Janus	God, beginnings, gates, transitions, time, duality, passages, endings

Symbol	Name	Meaning
	Juno (Hera)	Goddess, marriage, protector of women, fertility, childbirth, family
	Jupiter (Zeus)	God, the sky, lightning, thunder, law, order, justice
	Justitia (Astraea)	Goddess, justice, innocence, purity, precision

Symbol	Name	Meaning
	Justitia (Dike)	Goddess, justice, the spirit of moral order, fair judgment
	Justitia (Themis)	Goddess, divine law and order
	Juventas (Hebe)	Goddess, eternal youth, prime of life, forgiveness, cupbearer to the gods
	Latona (Leto)	Goddess, motherhood
	Lucina	Goddess, light, fertility

Magical Symbolism 6. *Astrological Symbols for Roman and Greek Deities*

Symbol	Name	Meaning
	Luna (Selene)	Goddess, the moon
	Mars (Ares)	God, battle, bravery, courage, war
	Melpomene	Muse, singing, melody, chorus, lament, tragedy

100

Magical Symbolism 6. Astrological Symbols for Roman and Greek Deities

Symbol	Name	Meaning
	Mercurius (Hermes)	God, boundaries, roads, travellers, thieves athletes, shepherds, commerce, speed, cunning, wit, sleep, divine messenger
	Metis	Goddess, wisdom, deep thought, magical cunning, skill, craft
	Minerva (Athena)	Goddess, poetry, medicine, strategic warfare, commerce, weaving, the crafts, wisdom, courage, inspiration, victory, war, law, civilization, bravery, heroism, protection, city state, family, justice, mathematics, science, technology, strength, strategy, the arts, and skill

Magical Symbolism   6. *Astrological Symbols for Roman and Greek Deities*

Symbol	Name	Meaning
	Mithras	God, agreement, pacts, oaths, light, all-seeing, protector of truth, guardian of cattle, the harvest, and the waters
	Moneta (Mnemosyne)	Goddess, memory, remembrance
	Morta (Atropos)	Goddess, fate, destiny, cutting the thread of human life
	Neptunus (Poseidon)	God, the seas, storms, earthquakes, horses

Magical Symbolism   6. Astrological Symbols for Roman and Greek Deities

Symbol	Name	Meaning
	Nona (Clotho, Klotho)	Goddess, fate, destiny, spinning the thread of human life
	Nox (Nyx)	Goddess, the night, power, beauty
	Ops (Rhea)	Goddess, plenty, fertility, the earth
	Orpheus	Prophet, music, poetry, the underworld
	Pax (Eirene)	Goddess, peace

Magical Symbolism 6. Astrological Symbols for Roman and Greek Deities

Symbol	Name	Meaning
	Phobos	God, fear, panic
	Pluto / Orcus / Dis Pater (Hades)	God, the underworld, the dead, punisher of broken oaths, the afterlife, mineral wealth

Magical Symbolism   6. Astrological Symbols for Roman and Greek Deities

Symbol	Name	Meaning
	Polyhymnia	Muse, sacred poetry, hymns, dance, eloquence, agriculture, pantomime, geometry, meditation
	Pomona	Wood Nymph, fruit, fruitful abundance
	Prometheus	God, fire, intelligence, forethought, crafty counsel, trickster
	Proserpina (Persephone)	Goddess, fertility, wine, spring, flowers, seasonal agriculture, life and death, the underworld

Magical Symbolism   6. *Astrological Symbols for Roman and Greek Deities*

Symbol	Name	Meaning
	Proteus	God, the sea, rivers, the changing nature of the sea, versatility, mutability, adaptability
	Psyche	Goddess, the soul
	Salacia (Amphitrite)	Goddess, the sea, salt water, the depths of the ocean

Magical Symbolism   *6. Astrological Symbols for Roman and Greek Deities*

Symbol	Name	Meaning
	Salus (Hygieia)	Goddess, good health, healing, cleanliness, sanitation, wellbeing, safety, salvation
	Saturnus (Cronus)	God, time, wealth, agriculture, the harvest, liberation, periodic renewal
	Serapis	God, abundance, agriculture, wealth, resurrection
	Silvia	Goddess, the forest

Magical Symbolism   *6. Astrological Symbols for Roman and Greek Deities*

Symbol	Name	Meaning
	Sol (Helios)	God, the sun, oaths, sight
	Styx	Goddess, river, the boundary between the earth and the underworld
	Tellus / Terra (Gaia)	Goddess, the earth, mother of all life
	Terpsichore	Muse, delight in dancing, dance, chorus

Symbol	Name	Meaning
	Tethys	Goddess, the sea, water, rivers, baths, pools
	Thalia	Muse, joy, comic poetry, idyllic poetry
	Theia	Goddess, sight, brilliance
	Triton	God, the sea, divine messenger

Magical Symbolism   6. Astrological Symbols for Roman and Greek Deities

Symbol	Name	Meaning
	Trivia (Hecate)	Goddess, boundaries, crossroads, witchcraft, ghosts
	Urania	Muse, astronomy, the stars, heaven
	Venus (Aphrodite)	Goddess, love, beauty desire, sexuality, pleasure, passion
	Vertumnus	God, change, seasons, plant growth, gardens, fruit trees, form changing

Magical Symbolism   6. *Astrological Symbols for Roman and Greek Deities*

Symbol	Name	Meaning
	Vesta (Hestia)	Goddess, hearth, home, family, fireplace, sacred fire, domesticity
	Victoria (Nike)	Goddess, victory

Magical Symbolism   6. *Astrological Symbols for Roman and Greek Deities*

Symbol	Name	Meaning
	Vulcanus (Hephaestus)	God, fire, metalwork, the forge, stone masonry, sculpture, technology, blacksmiths, volcanoes

7. Shields

These symbol shields are combinations of runes, galdrastafir, and astrological symbols linked by a theme or an idea, and set in varying degrees of symmetry into a 'shield' to protect the symbols and their combined meaning.

The number of possible combinations, configurations, and compositions of symbols into these shields is potentially limitless, all with their own unique character and significance.

7.1 Divine Inspiration

7.2 Fate and Destiny

7.3 Fertility

Magical Symbolism 7. Shields

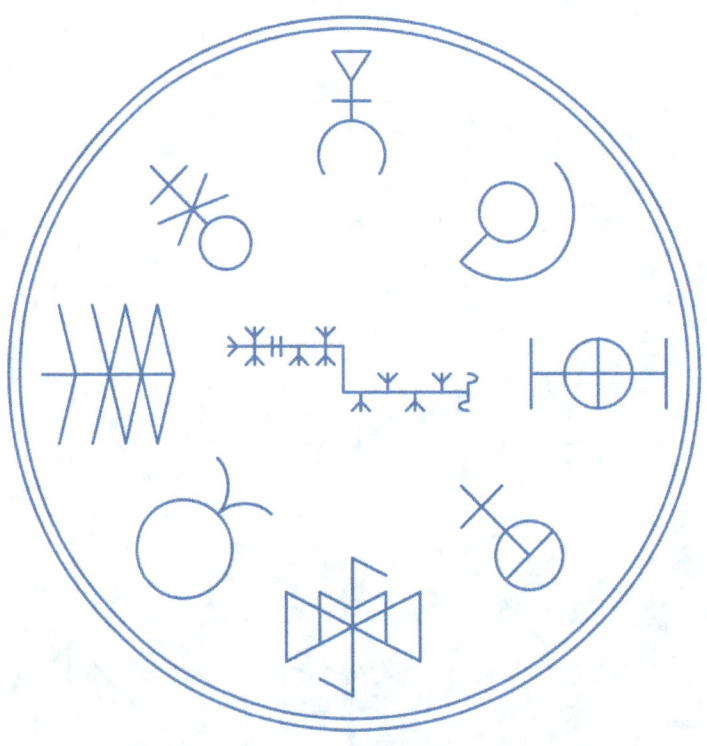

7.4 Health and Wellbeing

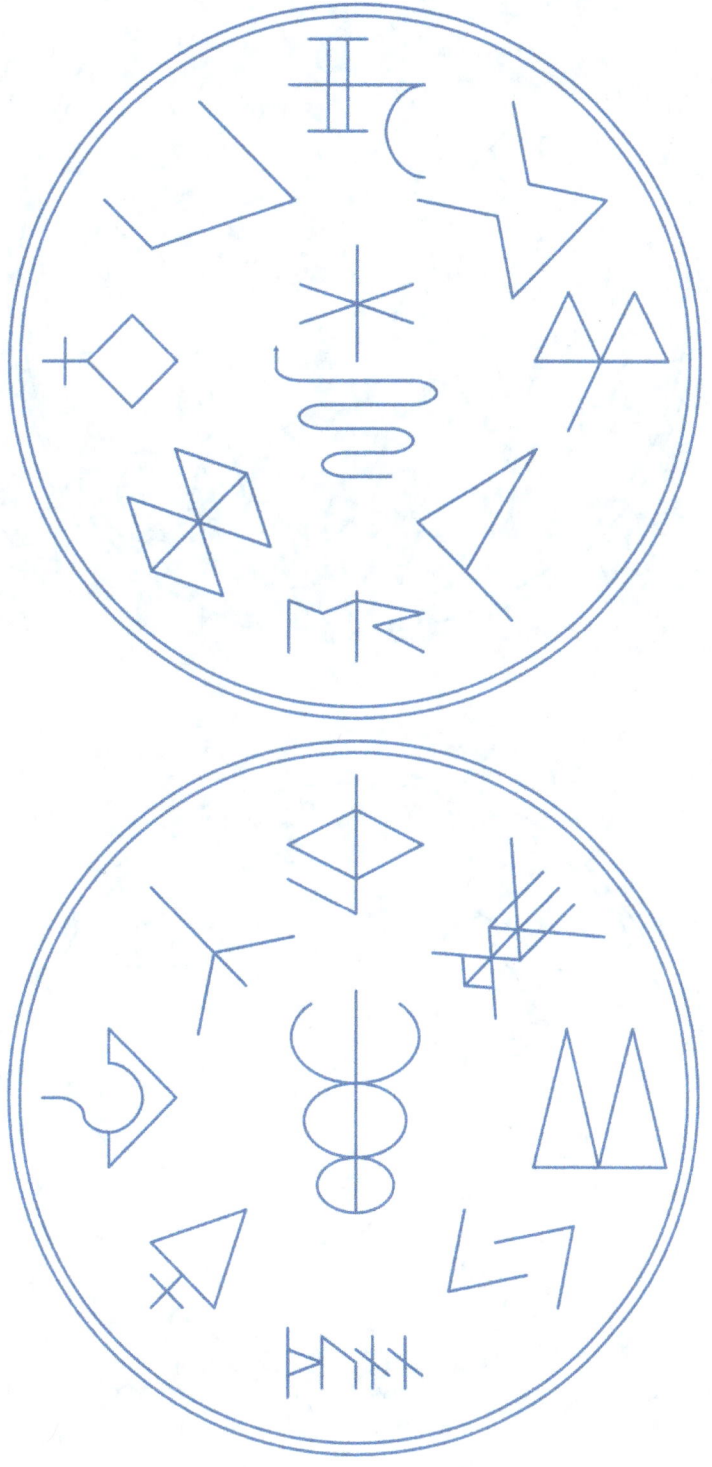

Magical Symbolism 7. Shields

7.5 Justice

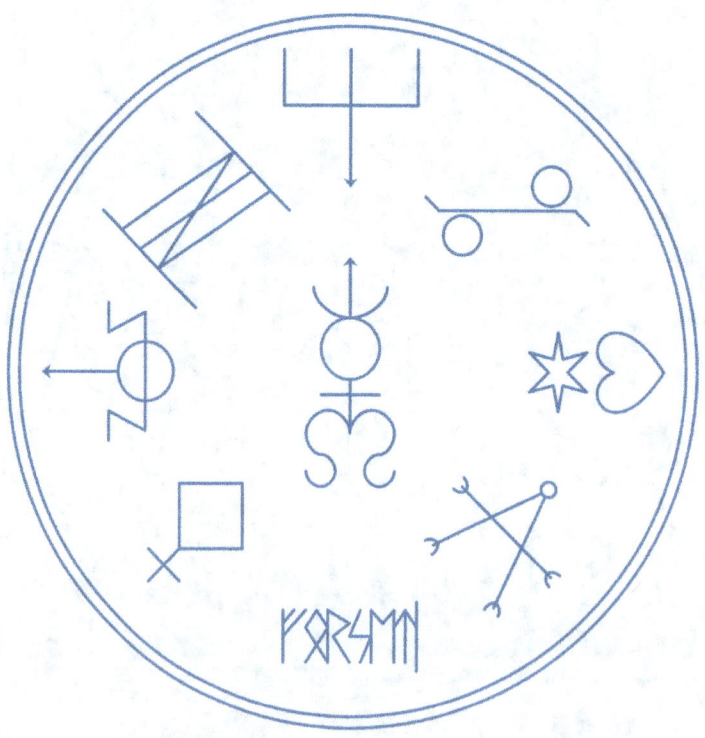

Magical Symbolism 7. Shields

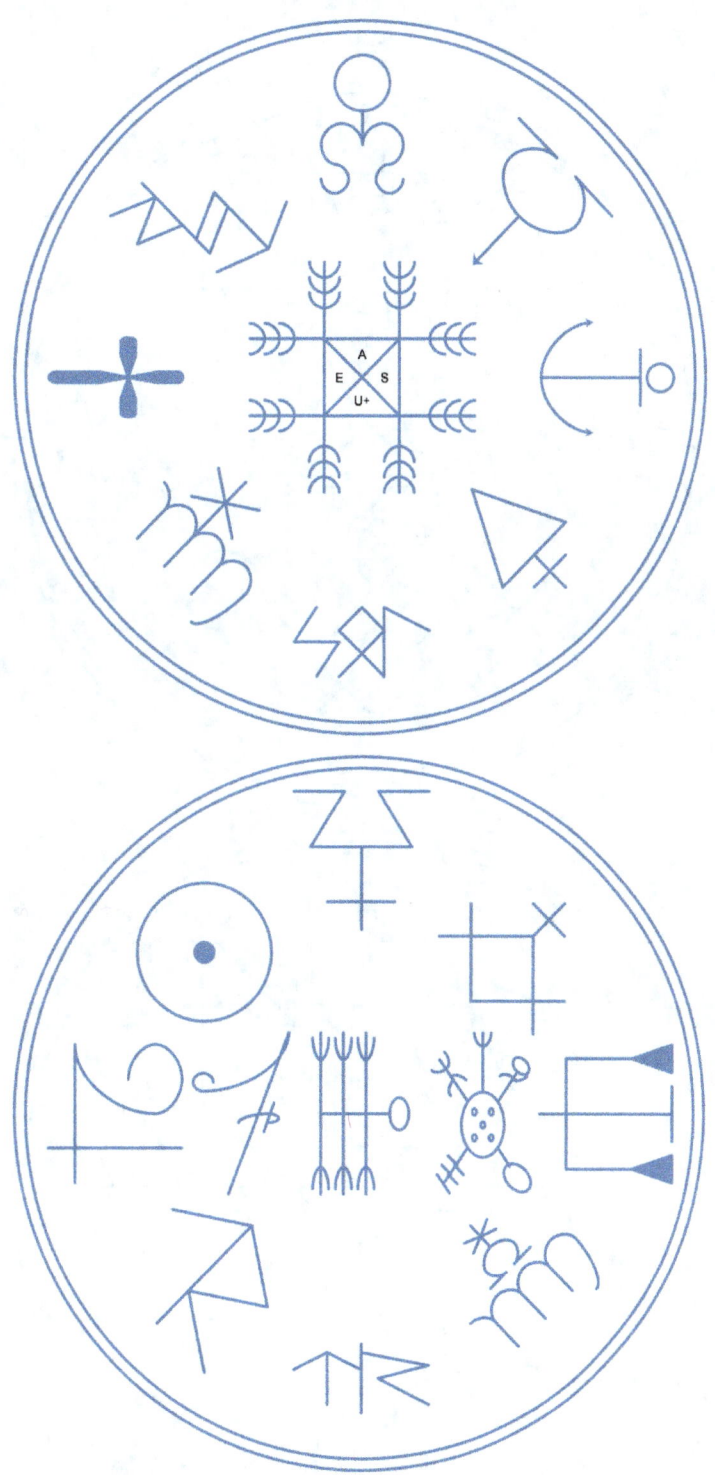

7.6 Love

7.7 Luck

7.8 Music and Art

7.9 Protection

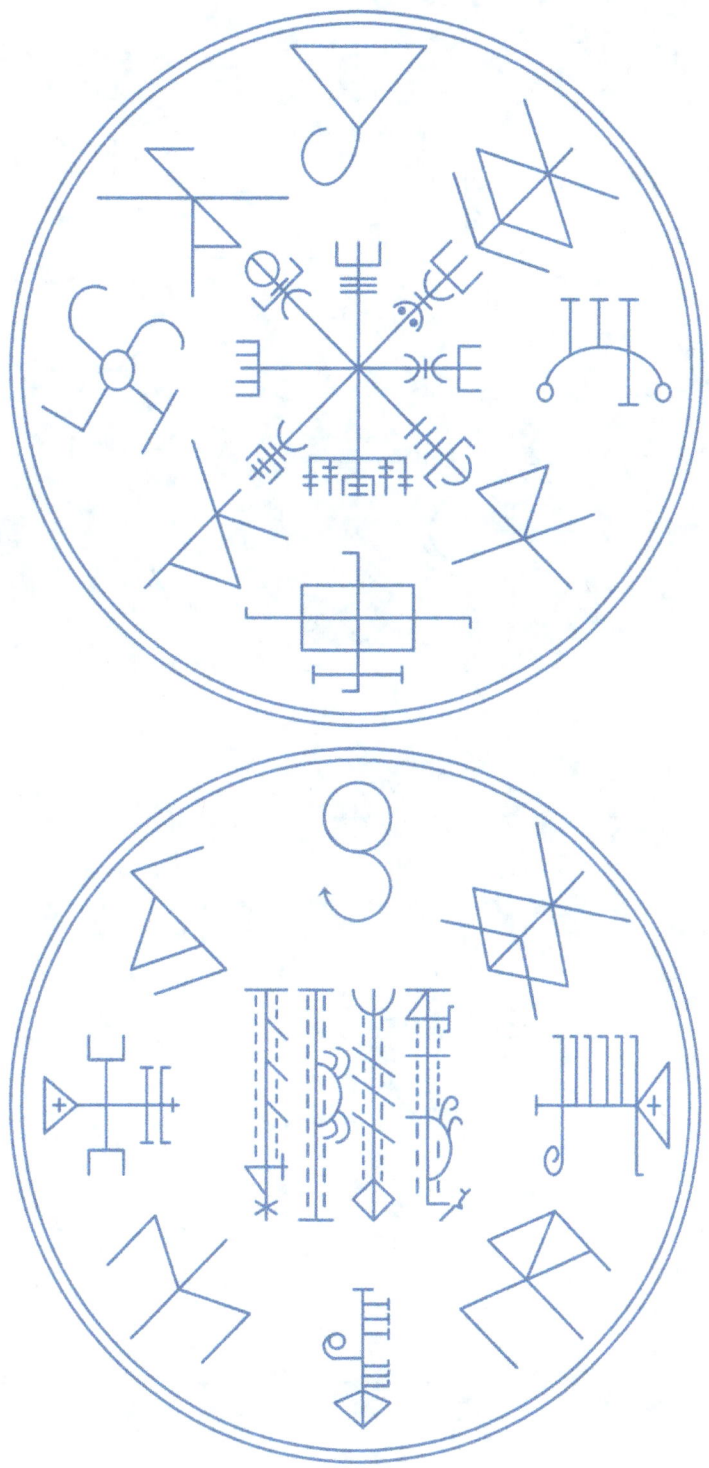

7.10 Resolving Conflict

7.11 Setting Intentions

7.12 Sleep and Dreams

7.13 Strength

7.14 Success and Victory

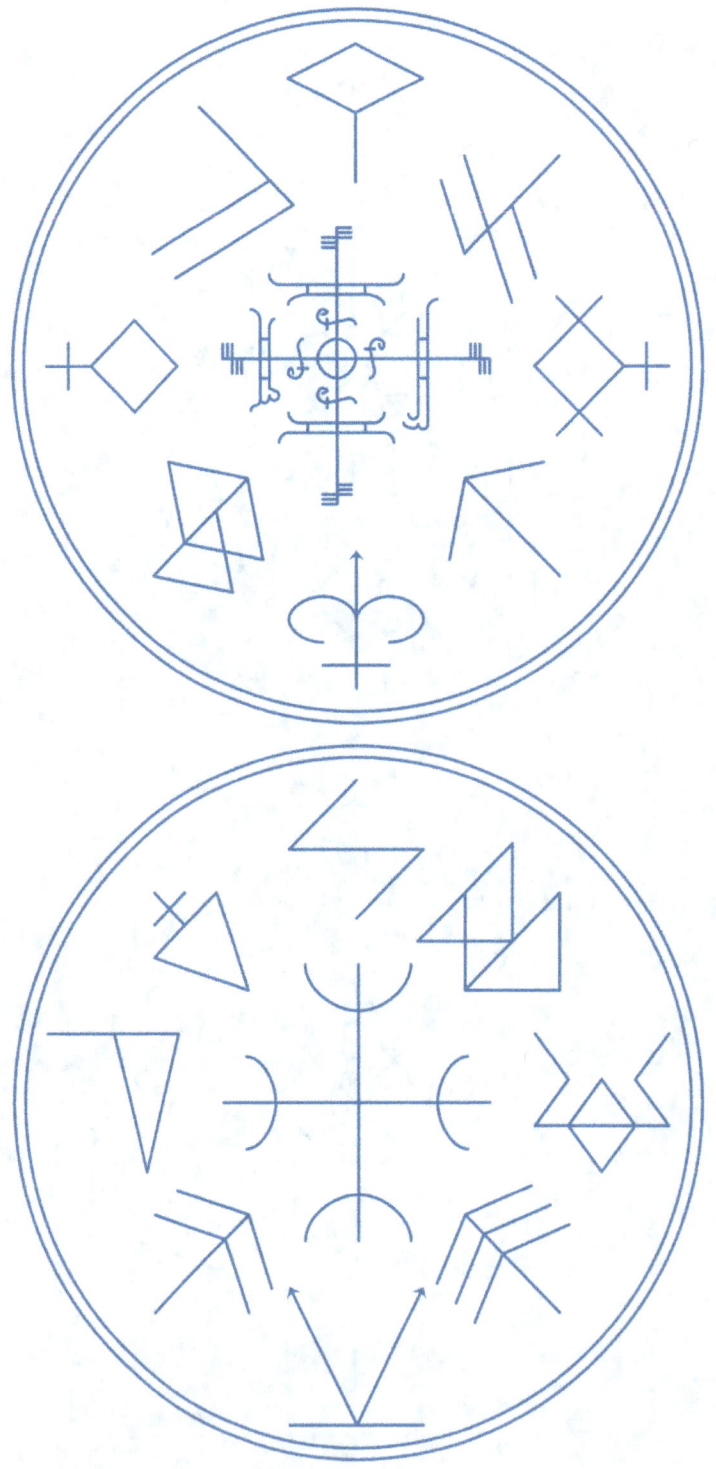

7.15 The Sea

7.16 Wealth

Magical Symbolism   7. Shields

7.17 Wisdom

Magical Symbolism 7. Shields

8. The Misuse of Runes: What to Avoid

For the last 120 years, runes have been misused, misrepresented, and misinterpreted to fit into systems of propaganda for extreme and objectionable political agendas. This form of cultural appropriation has done great damage in obscuring and twisting the original and true meanings of the runes, to the point where in some landscapes of public consciousness, runes are widely visually associated with Nazism and the horrors of World War 2, Neo-Nazism, far-right extremism, fascism, anti-semitism, racism, white supremacy, and hatred.

The seeds for this deeply problematic offshoot were sown in the early 20th century at a time of heightened nationalism, with a revival of interest in Germanic culture, mythology, runology, and the occult. The Austrian mysticist and Germanic revivalist Guido von List invented and devised the so-called 'Armanen Runes' (Armanen relating to Armanism, Ariosophy, and Aryanism). They consisted of 18 pseudo-runes which were based on the 16 runes of the Younger Futhark with adapted spellings and meanings, and two additional runes loosely based on those from the Anglo-Saxon Futhorc. They were first published in a periodical in 1906, and again as a standalone publication in 1908. The last rune called '*Gibor*' is not related to any historical runes, and is a '*Wolfsangel*' symbol, which particularly in this illustration appears alarmingly similar to the swastika.

Rune	Name	Rune	Name	Rune	Name
ᚡ	fa / F	ᚼ	hagal / hag / H	ᛒ	Bar / B
ᚢ	Ur / U	ᛐ	Nauth / Not / N	ᛚ	Laf / L
ᚦ	Thurs / Th (Þ)	ᛁ	Is / I	ᛉ	Man / M
ᛆ	Os / A (O)	ᛚ	Ar / A	ᛦ	Yr / Y
ᚱ	Rit / R	ᛌ	Sig / Sol / S	ᛖ	Eh / E
ᚴ	Ka / K	↑	Tyr / T	⌘	Gibor / Ge / Gi / G

Image Source: Wikipedia Creative Commons, Public Domain

The Armanen runes became influential in the Völkisch movement in Germany which promoted interest in Germanic folklore. They had already adopted the swastika as a supposed symbol of Germanic antiquity (a symbol found all over Eurasia as far back as 10,000 BCE, and documented in Sanskrit as far back as 500 BCE), and rejected values such as liberalism, democracy, socialism, and industrial capitalism. They associated these values with the Weimar Republic of Germany which they denounced as being 'un-German' and inspired by subversive Jewish influences. Nazism and Nazi occultism made widespread use of these symbols for propaganda, particularly in the SS (Schutzstaffel) where their use was systematised by Heinrich Himmler. The swastika is still used as a symbol of divinity in Hinduism, Buddhism, and Jainism, but in the western world it will never be able to shake off its association with Nazism, anti-Semitism, white supremacism, and evil.

Since the end of World War 2, continuing efforts have been made by various occultists and runologists to undo the damage done by the Nazi appropriation of runes. These efforts however are undermined by Neo-Nazi movements who have continued to use runes in their propaganda, and as an alternative script for tattoos containing such words and phrases as 'skinhead', 'hate', 'white power', etc. The appearance of runes in this context is understandably visually intimidating to those who cannot read them, and abhorrent to those who can.

In 2019, the government of Sweden discussed the idea of banning the use of runes because of their misappropriation by, and association with such groups. However this would have unfairly punished the far greater number of people who continue to use runes in accordance with the ancient traditions, as spiritual symbols of the interaction of humankind, the forces of nature, the gods, and the universe. It would be a tragedy if we were to relinquish two thousand years of linguistic and spiritual tradition because of the grossly misguided politically motivated actions of a few, the misunderstandings of some, and the lack of knowledge of others. The logic of this debate has also been transposed into a comparative notion of banning the use of the Arabic script because of its use by the militant Islamist group Islamic State (IS).

It is worth noting here which symbols have been misused and how, so that the reader may make careful and informed choices. With the right knowledge they should be well equipped to be able to explain with confidence what their symbol *actually* means, and what it definitely does *not* mean, highlighting the large degree of separation between original and misappropriated meaning. It is also worth noting that in designing the configuration and symmetry of runes that some unintended symbols may be inadvertently made or implied, further to the advice given in the Bindrunes section on Page 11.

Since the reader of this book will no doubt be interested in the full and true history of runes and Nordic symbols and their use for spiritual purposes, the last thing that they would want is to have designed their own rune stave only to have it misinterpreted by people who do not know the full history of the symbols, or worse still to be accused of belonging to a political movement or ideology that they do not belong to and would never wish to. From time to time there may be people who make such accusations or claims, understandably believing that they are actively doing a good thing by calling out evil wherever they see it. If the opportunity for an open and well informed debate and discussion is taken, a bridge of greater knowledge and understanding can be built whereupon it may be understood that the true evil lies in the corruption, distortion, and the taking over of that which is good for the purposes of evil. Context is everything, and half-knowledge is a dangerous thing.

Magical Symbolism   8. The Misuse of Runes: What to Avoid

Arrow Cross		The 'Arrow Cross' symbol comes from the Hungarian fascist political party known as the Arrow Cross Party, which was active during 1935-45. Since then, various neo-Nazis and white supremacists have used the symbol. In the United States, the 'Arrow Cross' has been used as the logo for a small Mississippi-based white supremacist group known as the Nationalist Movement (which called the image the 'Crosstar'). **Advice: avoid binding 'Tiwaz' or 'Tyr' runes into a stave with 4 points of symmetry to avoid association with this symbol.**
Eif		The 'Eif' rune is a rotated and reflected version of the 'Eihwaz' rune. During the early years of the SS it was used by Hitler's personal administrators, such as Rudolf Hess. **Advice: avoid turning an 'Eihwaz' rune onto its side to avoid association with this symbol.**
Ger		The 'Ger' rune was used to symbolise the communitarian ideal of the SS. The 11th SS Volunteer Panzergrenadier Division Nordland, a Waffen-SS unit, adopted the rune as a variant of its divisional insignia. **Advice: Avoid making 'Sowilo' runes too square, and make them narrower to avoid association with this symbol, but do not place two side by side.**
Hagal	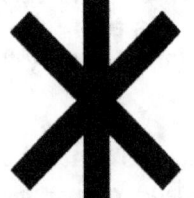	The Armanen version of the 'Hagal' rune was widely used in the SS for its symbolic representation of 'unshakeable faith' in Nazi philosophy according to Heinrich Himmler put it. It was used in SS weddings as well as on the SS-Ehrenring (death's head ring) worn by members of the SS. The rune was also used as division insignia of the 6th SS Mountain Division Nord. **Advice: lengthen the central stem at the top and the bottom so that the proportions are closer to the 'Haglaz' rune of the Younger Futhark to avoid association with this symbol.**
Heilszeichen		The Heilszeichen symbols appeared on the SS 'death's head' ring and were used to symbolise good fortune and success. **Advice: Avoid making the 'Sowilo' rune too narrow. Do not place two 'Sowilo' runes side by side. Avoid binding an upside down 'Fehu' rune to a 'Tyr' rune to avoid association with this symbol.**

Jera		The 'Jera' rune symbolises concepts such as the harvest or the passage of time. It is one of the less common runic symbols appropriated by modern white supremacists, perhaps because the Nazis do not appear to have used it. In the 2010s, however, white supremacists in Europe and the United States began to use the symbol. In Sweden, for example, the National Youth League (Förbundet Nationell Ungdom), a neo-Nazi group, adopted the Jera rune as its logo. In the United States, the rune began to appear on flyers and cards associated with the alt right segment of the white supremacist movement. Because the Jera rune is used by non-racists as well, including by adherents of modern pagan religions such as Asatru, one should not assume use of the symbol is racist but instead should only judge the symbol carefully in its specific context.
Ku Klux Klan		The triangular Ku Klux Klan symbol consists of what looks like a triangle within a triangle but which actually represents three letter K's aligned in a triangle and facing inwards. The same effect could be inadvertently achieved by creating a triangle of three inward facing 'Berkanaz' runes representing nurturing and motherhood. **Advice: Avoid intersecting lines that result in triangles. Avoid binding runes together with triangular shapes, such as 'Berkanaz' to avoid association with this symbol.**
Leben		The Armanen 'Lebensrune' or 'life rune' was based on the 'Algiz' or 'Elhaz' rune and was used by the Sturmabteilung, NSDAP and the SS. Because of the Nazi use of the symbol, later white supremacists continued to use the Life rune and it became very popular after the neo-Nazi National Alliance adopted the symbol as part of their logo. Since then, it has become a very common white supremacist symbol, used by neo-Nazis and other white supremacists. Because the Life Rune also continues to be used by non-racists, typically adherents of neo-pagan religions, one should not simply assume that a particular use of this symbol is racist, but should carefully judge it in its context.
Opfer		The 'Opfer' rune is a rotated version of the 'Eihwaz' rune. It was used by the Der Stahlhelm war veterans movement that eventually merged with the Sturmabteilung. The symbol was adopted by the Nazis after 1923 to commemorate the party members who died in Hitler's failed Beer Hall Putsch. **Advice: Avoid rotating an 'Eihwaz' rune onto its side to avoid association with this symbol.**

Othala

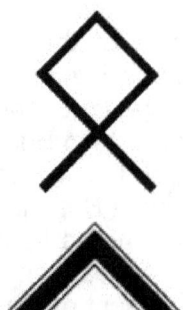

The 'Othala' rune from the Elder Futhark symbolised ancestry, heritage, and family. Its meaning was twisted to mean the protection of ethnic purity. During the Second World War it was used by the SS. Following World War II, white supremacists in Europe, North America, and elsewhere began using the 'Othala' rune. The variation of this rune with additional 'feet' or 'wings' is closely associated with its use by the SS. However, because it is part of the runic alphabet, the symbol can also be found in non-extremist contexts as well, especially runic writing and runestones used by non-racist pagans. Consequently, care should be taken to evaluate the symbol in the context in which it appears.

Both versions of this symbol have been depicted as an astrological symbol for Asteroid #3989 known as 'Odin' discovered on 8th September 1986 by P Jensen at the Brorfelde Observatory in Denmark. The name and number of this asteroid was allocated by the Minor Planet Center (MPC) which is part of the Smithsonian Astrophysical Observatory.

Advice: Avoid using 'feet' or 'wings' for this rune. Even though this variant has been used as an astrological symbol, it is still more closely associated with Nazism than the version without 'feet' or wings'. Its use has also been made illegal in Germany under the 'Strafgesetzbuch section 86a'.

SS Bolts

The SS Bolts are a common white supremacist / neo-Nazi symbol derived from Schutzstaffel (SS) of Nazi Germany. It is derived from the 'Sowilo' or 'sun' rune from the Elder Futhark. Following World War II, the SS bolts symbol was adopted by white supremacists and neo-Nazis worldwide. Most white supremacists use it in its Nazi form, as two bolt-like images with flattened ends. However, sometimes the symbol may have pointed bottom ends or pointed tops and bottoms. These variants of the SS bolts are most frequently associated with prison tattoos. The SS bolts are typically used as a symbol of white supremacy but there is one context in which this is not necessarily always so. Decades ago, some outlaw biker gangs appropriated several Nazi-related symbols, including the SS bolts, essentially as shock symbols or symbols of rebellion or non-conformity. Thus SS bolts in the context of the outlaw biker subculture does not necessarily denote actual adherence to white supremacy. However, because there are a number of racists and full-blown white supremacists within the outlaw biker subculture, sometimes it actually is used as a symbol of white supremacy. Often the intended use and meaning of the SS bolts in this context is quite ambiguous and difficult to determine. **Advice: Avoid placing two 'Sowilo' runes side by side to avoid association with this symbol.**

Tod		The Todesrune is the inverted version of the Armanen Lebensrune or 'life rune'. It was based on the 'Yr' rune, which originally meant 'yew'. It was used by the SS to represent death on documents and grave markers in place of the more conventional † symbol used for such purposes.
Tyr		The Tyr was based on the 'Tiwaz' rune, named after Týr, the god of single combat, victory and heroic glory in Norse mythology. It was widely used by the SS as a battle rune symbolising military leadership. The SS commonly used it in place of the Christian cross on the grave markers of its members. It was also used by graduates of the SA Reichsführerschule, which trained SS officers until 1934; they wore it on their upper left arms. It was adopted as an emblem by the 32nd SS Volunteer Grenadier Division 30 Januar, which was assembled from the members of SS schools in January 1945, as well as by the SS Recruitment and Training Department. Since World War II, neo-Nazis and other white supremacists continued to use the 'Tyr' rune in a racist context. The Tyr rune is one of the most common white supremacist appropriations of ancient runic symbols. Its popularity in part stems from the fact that it is considered by many to be the 'warrior rune'. Because today the Tyr rune continues to be used by non-racists as well, including members of various neo-pagan religions, one should not assume that use of the symbol is racist but instead should judge the symbol carefully in its specific context.
Valknut		The Valknot or 'knot of the slain' is an old Norse symbol that often represented the afterlife in carvings and designs. It is often considered a symbol of the Norse god Odin. Some white supremacists, particularly racist Odinists, have appropriated the Valknot to use as a racist symbol. Often they use it as a sign that they are willing to give their life to Odin, generally in battle. Non-racist pagans may also use this symbol, so one should carefully examine it in context rather than assume that a particular use of the symbol is racist.
Wolfsangel		The Wolfsangel is an ancient symbol that was believed to be able to ward off wolves. It appeared as part of the divisional insignia of several Waffen-SS units, including the notorious 2nd SS "Das Reich" Panzer Division. As a result, it became a symbol of choice for neo-Nazis in Europe and the United States. In the United States, the neo-Nazi group Aryan Nations incorporated the Wolfsangel into their logo. **Advice: Avoid inadvertently making or implying this symbol by having any lines intersecting a 'Sowilo' or 'Ihwaz' rune to avoid association with this symbol.**

www.ingramcontent.com/pod-product-compliance
Lightning Source LLC
Chambersburg PA
CBHW051413070526
44584CB00023B/3411